Beyond the Grave

Love and Immortality

Floyd Vernon Chandler

W0010431

RESOURCE *Publications* · Eugene, Oregon

BEYOND THE GRAVE
Love and Immortality

Resource Publications
An Imprint of Wipf and Stock Publishers
199 W. 8th Ave., Suite 3
Eugene, OR 97401
www.wipfandstock.com

ISBN 13: 978-1-60608-938-5

Manufactured in the U.S.A.

*This collection of sermons and reflections is
Dedicated in loving honor to my mother,
Ledora Elizabeth "Betty" Broome McDonald.*

Contents

PART TWO   REFLECTIONS

Preface

THIS COLLECTION OF SERMONS and reflections has been years in the making. The title of this book, *Beyond the Grave: Love and Immortality*, is the essence of much of my theology regarding immortality. The title is taken from a sermon written and delivered for Universalist Convocation 1994 hosted by the Westfield Center Universalist Church, Westfield Center, Ohio. Although this book has been written with the thought that most readers will be those of the Universalist and Unitarian Universalist faith traditions, I hope this book will find a home with many other progressive and liberal religious seekers who are looking for a spiritual path and religious faith that makes sense in our modern world.

I believe there are many valid spiritual paths to enlightenment, holiness, and salvation. The essence of the mystery we call God is the same for the Christian and Jew, the Buddhist and Hindu, the Muslim and the Native American. It is akin to the story of five blind men touching different parts of a huge elephant. Each man's description and understanding of the elephant varied based upon the location of his touch. It is not so important the doctrine or dogma of our different faith paths. For me, the importance of any religion is determined by how much our respective spiritual paths lead us to grow in love and compassion for one another and for all other life forms on this planet.

Although the theme of immortality is represented in many of the sermons and reflections, other theological topics and life reflections are included in this collection. These sermons and reflections cover a twenty-five-year period. Most of the reflections in this collection have appeared in the *Universalist Herald*, which has the distinction of being "The Oldest Continuously Published Liberal Religious Magazine in North America." My association with the *Universalist Herald* dates back to May 1984 when I met Editor Haynie Summers at Harmony Universalist Church in Senoia, Georgia, prior to my departure for a one-year tour of duty as an army chaplain in the Republic of Korea. It was at this particular Sunday morning service that I met William H. "Bill" Balkan, who was currently serving as president of the Georgia Universalist Convention. My friend and colleague the Rev. Rhett Baird, who delivered the sermon at Harmony Universalist Church that Sunday morning, introduced me to both Haynie and Bill. Following the morning service, Haynie asked me to consider writing occasional articles for the *Universalist Herald* and I agreed to his request. Unfortunately, it was shortly after my arrival in Korea that I learned of Haynie's death. A few weeks after Haynie's death, the *Herald* board of trustees named Bill Balkan interim editor of the *Universalist Herald*, and the board later made the position a permanent one for Bill. I began writing for the *Herald* in 1984 while stationed in Korea, and I later served as associate editor, editor, board member, and chairperson of the *Herald* board. It is interesting how a chance encounter in May 1984 led to an over twenty-five-year association with some wonderful individuals I came to know as *Universalist Herald* subscribers, writers, board members, and editors. My involvement with the *Universalist Herald* has been a significant aspect of my ministry as a Unitarian Universalist minister.

I have tried my best to cite in the bibliography all original sources for quotes or references. Any quotes not listed from original sources in the bibliography were taken from Glendon Harris's *LectionAid* and *Pulpit Resources*. Otherwise, if I missed any source in citing quotations or references, it was unintentional.

My thanks to Wipf and Stock Publishers for considering and accepting this manuscript for publication under their Resource Publications imprint. Also, special thanks to Christian Amondson, Assistant Managing Editor at Wipf and Stock, for working with me during the initial phases of preparing this manuscript for publication. Thanks as well to Jim Tedrick, managing editor, and Diane Farley, editorial administrator, for their assistance in preparing this manuscript for publication. And very special thanks to my good friend and colleague, the Rev. Dr. John Morgan, for introducing me to Christian Amondson and recommending to Wipf and Stock that they consider *Beyond the Grave: Love and Immortality* for publication. Collections of sermons are not usually bestsellers. I am delighted that Wipf and Stock apparently believe that there is a market for what I have written.

Introduction

IN 2008 I HIT the big 55. Now as I write this introduction, I am several months past my fifty-sixth birthday. Everything I was ever told about life speeding by as you get older is true. It seems like it was only a couple of years ago when I hit the big 40! Also, it is true that life is what you do while you are trying to decide what it is you really want to do with your life. You wake up one morning and realize that most of your life is over! Working and serving for over thirty-three years as a Unitarian Universalist minister was one of the things I did while trying to decide what I really wanted to do with my life.

Whether I planned it this way or not, life has been good. The past nine years have been a special blessing for me. Since meeting my wife, Nataliya, in June of 2000, my life has been such an adventure and so much fun. I am enjoying life more than at any time since becoming an adult. Life is good! Now, at age fifty-six, I am a father for the first time. Will wonders never cease? My two younger brothers, Thomas and Joseph, are already grandfathers!

Maybe it was the big 55 or maybe it was the birth of our daughter, Katerine Elizabeth, on July 3, 2008, or maybe it was the fact that I was afraid of losing these sermons and reflections, since most of them were saved on the hard drive of a 1989 Macintosh computer. But for whatever the reason, I have felt a real urge for months to put together this collection of sermons and reflections from my years as a Unitarian Universalist minister.

I've had a varied ministry. I've served parish ministries in Brewton, Alabama; Clinton, North Carolina; Kinston, North Carolina, Seven Springs, North Carolina; and Newberry, South Carolina. All of my parish ministries have been with Universalist heritage Unitarian Universalist congregations. Along with parish ministry, I served for over thirty-two years as a chaplain in the U.S. Army Reserve, which included almost fourteen years of active duty. My active duty included stateside tours at Fort Wadsworth, New York; Fort Riley, Kansas; and Fort Jackson, South Carolina. My overseas tours of duty included the countries of Albania, Bosnia, Bulgaria, Croatia, Germany, Hungary, Korea, Kosovo, Macedonia, and Japan. While mobilized for six-teen months of active duty in Germany in 2003 to 2004, I served as consult-ing minister to the English-speaking Unitarian Universalist Congregation of Heidelberg. Along with my eleven years of parish ministry at Red Hill Universalist Church in Clinton, North Carolina, I worked full-time as a correctional chaplain (five years with the South Carolina Department of Corrections and three years with the North Carolina Department of Corrections.) Working with inmates and their families has been one of my most rewarding ministries. I've included one of my "prison sermons" in this collection. Variations of several of these sermons were also delivered in prison and military settings. When using the sermon in a non-Universalist or non-Unitarian Universalist setting, I simply deleted all references to Universalism, Unitarianism, or Unitarian Universalism.

You will note that I often refer to "Universalist" rather than "Unitarian Universalist" in my sermons. Let me explain. I think I would have been more at home with late-nineteenth-century Unitarianism or mid-twen-tieth-century Universalism than I am with contemporary Unitarian Universalism. In a nutshell, nineteenth-century Unitarianism differed from mainline Christianity because of their rejection of the doctrine of the Trinity. Unitarians did not believe that Jesus and God were the same. Most Unitarians believed Jesus to be a great teacher or prophet, but not a deity. Universalists differed from mainline Christianity primarily due to their rejection of the notion of an everlasting hell in the afterlife. Universalists equated God with love, and they did not believe a loving God would send any soul to an everlasting hell. Both Unitarians and Universalists rejected the notion of the Bible as the infallible word of God. Don't get me wrong! Unitarians and Universalists value the Holy Bible as a source of religious inspiration and wisdom, as we treasure the inspiration and wisdom found in holy books from other religious traditions. However, Unitarians and Universalists (as well as many other progressive Christians and those of other faith traditions) do not consider the King James Version or any re-vised version of the Holy Bible as the inerrant and infallible Word of God. The sources of the Holy Bible are varied and it is the product of various traditions and human interpretations. However, our lack of affirming the Holy Bible as inerrant and infallible does not discount this great book as a wonderful source of religious inspiration and spiritual wisdom.

Although I was raised a United Methodist, was the son of a United Methodist minister (now deceased), and even received deacon ordination in the South Carolina Conference of the United Methodist Church, I think my theology has been Unitarian and Universalist since my early teens. The Christian doctrines regarding the Trinity, salvation, atonement, and hell never made sense to me, and after a total of three years of graduate theological studies and four years of doctoral theological studies, I must confess that these basic Christian theological doctrines still make no sense to me! Even as a child, I could never understand how a loving God could send devout and loving Buddhists, Hindus, Jews, or Muslims to an everlasting punishment in hell simply because they did not believe Jesus was the Son of God. Such a God did not sound very loving, kind, or just to me!

The American writer and Unitarian minister Ralph Waldo Emerson will always be a spiritual mentor for me. I can very much relate to Emerson's religious thought. Emerson's concept of God as expressed in his essay "The Oversoul" is very similar to my own thoughts about the mystery we call "God."

Moreover, I must admit that I find much humor and truth in the religious skepticism of Samuel Clemens, alias Mark Twain. In a letter Mark Twain wrote to the San Francisco *Alta California* in 1865, he says, "A religion that comes of thought, and study, and deliberate conviction, sticks best. The revivalized convert who is scared in the direction of heaven because he sees hell yawn suddenly behind him, not only regains confidence when his scare is over, but is ashamed of himself for being scared, and often becomes more hopelessly and malignantly wicked than he was before." In "The Lowest Animal," Mark Twain writes,

> Man is a Religious Animal. He is the only Religious Animal. He is the only animal that has the True Religion . . . several of them. He is the only animal that loves his neighbor as himself and cuts his throat if his theology isn't straight. He has made a graveyard of the globe in trying his honest best to smooth his brother's path to happiness and heaven. . . . The higher animals have no religion. And we are told that they are going to be left out in the Hereafter. I wonder why? It seems questionable taste.

I do resonate with much of Mark Twain's religious observations!

Lastly, I wish to mention a contemporary theologian and good friend with whom I have much admiration and respect, Dr. A. J. Mattill Jr. Although Dr. Mattill and I differ in our views regarding the afterlife, I find Dr. Mattill's 1987 publication *A New Universalism for a New Century* a very positive and practical religious credo to match humanity's modern understanding of the world. At the heart of Mattill's theology is "fourfold reverence": reverence for truth; reverence for beauty; reverence for life; and reverence for the mystery of the universe. Dr. Mattill, who received his PhD from Vanderbilt University, is a theologian who very much practices his theology in his daily life. In his section regarding reverence for life, Dr. Mattill makes a convincing argument that every living thing has a powerful will to live. As the Golden Rule teaches that we should do unto others as we desire others to do unto us, Dr. Mattill applies the Golden Rule to all sentient beings. He expresses his belief that any true religion embraces the value of compassion for all things that have life and that harmlessness to all living things is the highest religion and is perhaps the only true religion. A. J. and his spouse, M. E., live an intentionally simple life on a small farm near Gordo, Alabama, where they practice organic gardening and follow a vegan lifestyle. They don't even own a television! I was honored to play a role in the 2008 reprinting of *A New Universalism for a New Century* and as I write this introduction, copies of this second printing are still available via the Universalist Herald Publishing Company. Information for ordering a copy can be found at the *Universalist Herald's* website: www.universalist-herald.net

Since the 1961 consolidation of the American Unitarian Association and the Universalist Church of America, Unitarian Universalism has become a very diverse religious organization comprised of a hodgepodge of liberal religious theologies and philosophies. I enjoy my involvement with Unitarian Universalism. I am always stimulated by the intellect found in Unitarian Universalist gatherings. Some of the most intelligent and educated folks in the world can be found in Unitarian Universalist congregations and fellowships. Although my brain finds more than ample intellectual stimulation at Unitarian Universalist events, I have found that my soul and spirit often go lacking. It is among the Universalists within Unitarian Universalism that I find my spiritual home. During my parish ministry to Universalist-heritage congregations and my involvement with the Universalist Convocations organization, I have found my soul and spirit nourished. I have met some wonderful Universalists over the past thirty-three years, and I was fortunate to have many of them within my congregations. To all those Universalists, both living and dead, who have touched my life and taught me so much about love and the "religion of Jesus" by your examples, I express my gratitude.

As someone who seriously considered applying for conscientious objector status as an eighteen-year-old, I am a bit surprised that I completed a military career that spanned over thirty-two years. On September 1, 2007, I retired from the U.S. Army Chaplain Corps. The military has afforded me some wonderful opportunities to travel, and I value the unique perspective one gains regarding one's own culture when viewed from a foreign land. I especially appreciated my work with international peace-keeping forces in the Balkans. I made some great friendships with chaplains from other NATO nations during my time in the former Yugoslavia. I count among my best friends several men and women with whom I have served in Army Reserve units and active duty assignments.

However, not all of my military duty was satisfying. Now that I am retired from the military, I can confess that I was opposed to the Iraq War from the very beginning. I never liked the way the Bush/Cheney administration rushed to war without the support of the United Nations and our NATO allies. My military service during the Iraq War was my most difficult time in uniform. I felt much emotional turmoil over what I came to believe was an unjust and probably an illegal military action. I was appalled when I learned that my beloved nation had decided to discard the Geneva Conventions, and it gave me great sorrow to learn that the Bush/Cheney administration advocated torture against "detainees" at various military and CIA-operated prisons. I often considered resigning my commission or requesting early retirement since so-called Operation Iraqi Freedom was launched in 2003, but I didn't. Maybe I should have.

My heart does go out to the American soldiers who have served and are serving in Iraq. American soldiers and their family members are making tremendous sacrifices as a result of this war that is now in its sixth year. The frequent and lengthy deployments that many of our soldiers are experiencing are taking a tremendous emotional toll upon both our soldiers and their family members.

Living outside the United States for most of the past nine years has given me a unique perspective upon the life that I once lived in the United States. Traveling abroad and spending at least one semester living in a foreign country should be a core requirement for earning a college degree. I've come to observe that the American values of liberty and freedom are mostly myths. They really are! In the United States, freedom and liberty are directly related to wealth. If you have wealth, you have freedom and liberty. I admit that in most countries, freedom and liberty are somewhat related to individual wealth, but nowhere like the United States of America do most of a nation's citizens seem to be in denial over this reality of economic justice. If you are unemployed or are a working-class American with no wealth, you have little, if any, freedom or liberty. Most working-class Americans live as indentured servants with constant fears of losing medical coverage (or the consequences of having no medical insurance), unemployment, foreclosure of homes, and/or inadequate funds for retirement. I make reference to some of these concerns in my sermon "More Bricks, But No Straw: Reflections on Work in the United States," which I wrote and later delivered at Clayton Memorial Unitarian Universalist Church in Newberry, South Carolina, in March of 2005. Unfortunately, many of the statistics I cite in this 2005 sermon have only worsened over the past four years.

I am no Marxist, but neither am I frightened by some aspects of socialism. Unbeknown to many Americans, socialism is not communism. It has been my observation that the citizens of Western European nations with various forms of socialized medicine are much more satisfied with their medical care than is the case with the majority of citizens in the United States! It is the lobbying of U.S. drug companies and medical insurance companies that have resulted in the scare tactics that frighten so many Americans concerning government-assisted universal health care. Face it: neither medical doctors nor their patients are happy with the current health care system in the United States. We need change and we need it now!

I do believe in the free market system. I invest in the U.S. and international stock markets and have accumulated what little wealth I possess from stock market investing. However, I think the events of the past few years clearly demonstrate that our free market system requires both transparency and regulation. I do believe the American capitalist system must move towards one that provides stronger safety nets for the working class and poor than what has been the case in the United States these past several decades. We need a compassionate capitalism. Working Americans must receive living wages. Our current minimum wage is nowhere near a living wage!

Working two or three jobs just to pay the rent and provide food for the table with neither job providing family medical coverage does not make for a balanced lifestyle. For most Americans, work (or looking for employment) is the only life we know. Family time, friends, hobbies, recreation, vacations, spiritual enrichment, cultural events, and so forth, are either low priorities or nonexistent for most Americans. The typical working-class lifestyles of most Americans are not very healthy ones! The disparity of wealth between the "haves" and the "have-nots" in the United States is outrageous and an international embarrassment. Equally embarrassing is the United States' health care system. As I write this sentence, it is estimated that over 47 million Americans are currently without medical insurance. Our senior citizens should not have to choose between using their meager funds to purchase either food or prescription medications, yet many do.

It is my hope that as we recover from our current severe economic recession, a new America will emerge that will be quite different from the America that was based primarily upon greed, materialism, and the exploitation of the working class. May this new America be a democracy founded upon compassionate capitalist principles. We must close the enormously large gap between the "haves" and the "have-nots." Hard-working Americans deserve living wages!

The planet we are leaving for our children and grandchildren is not a pretty sight. Human-induced climate change is a fact. The Intergovernmental Panel on Climate Change (IPCC) has concluded that the Earth's global warming is caused by green house gas emissions and that the warming trend will continue. Some of the climate changes are irreversible. Even if all green house gas emissions ceased immediately, certain global changes are inevitable. The Earth's average temperature will warm between 1.9 and 4.6 degrees Celsius in the next ninety years. Sea ice is projected to shrink in both the Arctic and Antarctic, and it is very possible that Arctic late-summer sea ice will disappear almost entirely by the latter part of the twenty-first century. Hot extremes, heat waves, and heavy precipitation events will continue to become more frequent. It is likely that future tropical cyclones will become more intense, with larger peak wind speeds and heavier precipitation. Certain drought-prone areas are likely to resemble deserts. Sea levels are projected to rise an amount between just under four inches to just under three feet before we reach the year 2100. These climate changes will have an enormous impact upon civilizations on our planet. Embracing a theology that includes compassion and respect for all life is a necessity if human life is to continue on Earth. Caring for our environment must take priority over the greed and materialism that contributes so much to the exploitation of Earth's resources.

Shifting gears, I want to add a few additional comments regarding my eight years as a correctional chaplain. Providing ministry to inmates was the most rewarding of my thirty-three years as a Unitarian Universalist minister. Before beginning correctional chaplaincy, I never dreamed that I would one day make such a statement concerning prison ministry. I must admit that working with a few of my fellow correctional employees and dealing with the correctional bureaucracy were anything but rewarding, but providing ministry to inmates was immensely satisfying.

Although the United States leads the world as the nation with the highest percentage of its citizens incarcerated, the plight of inmates and their families is one of which most Americans know little. The misleading stereotypical image of the men and women serving sentences behind prison bars is distorted by Hollywood filmmakers and "get-tough-on-crime" politicians seeking public office. Yes, there are some mean and scary folks serving long sentences in our nation's prisons, but they are a minority. Once you get to know the men and women known as "inmates," you quickly realize that but for the grace of God there go you and I.

Many Americans would like to believe that folks are either good or bad, and if only we could lock up all the bad people, the world would be safe. If only it were that simple! Alexander Solzhenitsyn in the *Gulag Archipelago* wrote: "If only there were evil people somewhere insidiously committing evil deeds, and it were necessary only to separate them from the rest of us and destroy them. But the line dividing good and evil cuts through the heart of every human being and who is willing to destroy a piece of his own heart?"

I never found anything resembling a "country club prison," and I doubt that such an entity exists anywhere in our nation except in the imagination of a few of our politicians and the citizens who vote for them. Life behind bars is harsh. Many Americans entering our prisons are forgotten by family and friends. Marriages rarely survive sentences of five or more years. Every hour of an inmate's daily routine is regimented. And, unfortunately, many inmates must live in constant fear of other inmates. Rape, assault, robbery, and extortion are not uncommon in prison.

Most of my time as a prison chaplain was spent in counseling. The counseling I have experienced with inmates was rich in both content and depth. Once inmates know that you care and are "for real," they will often bare their souls in telling their stories. It is amazing to me how many inmates have never had anyone just listen to their stories. The depth and willingness to risk that inmates have displayed as they have shared with me their life stories far exceeds any of the pastoral conversations I have had as a parish minister or a military chaplain. There are recurring themes that I heard over and over again as I listened to their stories: severe physical and/or sexual abuse as children, poverty, chemical addiction, and/or illiteracy. (Test scores reveal that the average South Carolina inmate functions on a sixth grade level.) Sad, but true, prisons are now the "institution of last resort" for many of our mentally ill. In one prison where I worked, approximately fifty percent of the inmates had been diagnosed with severe mental disorders requiring daily psychotropic medication.

It might surprise you to know that some of the nicest and most well-mannered folks you will ever meet in prison are those who are incarcerated on murder and manslaughter convictions. This is especially true with homicides related to crimes of passion involving a spouse or significant other or the lover of a spouse or significant other.

I have come to see that American justice is not very just. Those who are able to afford lawyers are less likely to go to prison than are those who must rely on public defenders. The more money you have to pay a lawyer, the less likely you are to go to prison.

The greatest rewards in working with inmates are the relationships that are established and the genuine appreciation that inmates express for you and your ministry. Often I joined inmates for food and fellowship in the prison cafeteria. At least twice a week, I'd spend an hour or so walking around the prison recreation yard with several of the inmates as we discussed theology or current events or as we reminisced about the past. I have been awed by the spirituality and spiritual consciousness of some of the inmates whom I came to know. One of my inmate "mentors" was quite influential in my decision to follow a vegetarian diet. (He introduced me to the book *Diet for a New America* by John Robbins.) Another inmate friend made me a true believer in the power of prayer.

Although I believe that a few folks in prison are actually innocent of the crimes for which they have been convicted, the vast majority of the inmates are guilty of the crimes that brought them to prison. Regardless of the crime, they remain human beings with feelings not unlike those of us who are fortunate enough to live outside prison walls. In my work in corrections, two adages guided my ministry with inmates: "Except by the grace of God go you and I," and "Do unto others as you would have them do unto you." I have also come to have a much greater appreciation for the words of

Jesus in Matthew 25: "Then the ones who pleased the Lord will ask, 'When did we give you something to eat or drink? When did we welcome you as a stranger or give you clothes to wear or visit you while you were sick or in jail?' The king will answer, 'Whenever you did it for any of my people, no matter how unimportant they seemed, you did it for me'" (Matt 25:37–40).

It does seem that I have become more of a social activist in my later years. Advocating for issues related to economic justice, accessible and affordable health care, global warming, the environment, and animal rights have become real passions for me.

The treatment farm animals receive in our factory farming method of raising meat for consumption is nothing less than evil. It is such an irony to me that the same individuals who cry "jail time" for persons who mistreat pet dogs or pet cats show no ethical concerns regarding the immense suffering and torture that cattle, hogs, chickens, and turkeys must endure from birth to slaughter in our factory farming industries. I do try to take advantage of any and every opportunity to educate folks to the evils of factory farming, although I know my actions have alienated many who prefer to remain ignorant or in denial regarding the horrors by which their meat dish makes it to their dining room table. I recall the quote by Ralph Waldo Emerson: "You have just dined, and however scrupulously the slaughterhouse is concealed in the great distance of miles, there is complicity." If you buy the meat products of factory farming, you are supporting this evil system just as much as those who own and manage these industries. Don't kid yourself: Ninety-nine percent of meat products found in all major grocery chains are produced via factory farming. However, there are many other valid reasons for switching to a meat-free diet, and I touch on some of these reasons in my reflection "Everyday Fear Factors of a Meat-Based Diet." A wonderful book I recommend to any of you who might like to further explore the many negative issues surrounding a meat-based diet (and the many positive reasons for following a meat-free diet) is Dr. Will Tuttle's *World Peace Diet*.

I hope you enjoy this collection of writings. And if you don't enjoy them, it is my wish that you will at least find them thought provoking. It would be nice to learn that some of my thoughts and reflections resonated with readers. I welcome your comments!

Floyd Vernon Chandler, III
Trippstadt, Germany
July 9, 2009

PART ONE

Sermons

Beyond the Grave: Love and Immortality

1 John 4:7–8; 1 Corinthians 13:12–13

THERE IS A STORY of a married couple who have an argument that is serious enough for the wife to storm out of the house, vowing never to return. On the back steps, she nearly trips over something she has never seen before. It is an Aladdin's lamp. She picks it up, rubs it gently, and, sure enough, out pops a Genie.

"I am at your command," the Genie says, "I will grant you three wishes for whatever you desire. Name it and it's yours." Naturally, she is overjoyed. But the Genie tempers her enthusiasm: "I know about the fight between you and your husband. I must tell you," the Genie cautions, "that whatever you get, your husband will get twice as much." The wife isn't too thrilled about that, but what can she say? She agrees to play by the rules, knowing that her husband will get double whatever she asks for.

"First," she says, "I would like a million dollars." Poof! Just like that a million dollars lay at her feet." She leaps for joy, but comes back to earth when the Genie reminds her that the husband she despises just received two million dollars. "Are you sure you want to go on?" the Genie asks.

"Sure," she says, with a little less enthusiasm. "Next, I'd like a pile of diamonds, three feet high." Poof! Right next to the money, appears a mound of sparkling diamonds, a yard high. "I don't want to dampen your fun," the Genie cautions, "but your husband is sitting in his Lazy Boy recliner with a pile of diamonds on both sides of his arm rests and two million dollars lying at his feet. Maybe you'd like to forego your third and final wish?"

The wife thinks about that for a moment or two, but then says, "No, Genie, I'd like that one last wish. What I want you to do—is scare me half to death."

There is another story of two teenage boys discussing the recent death of a rather wealthy widow. One boy asks the other "Well, how much do you suppose she left?" The other boy responded, "Are you kidding? She left it all."

How many times have we heard the statement "You can't take it with you"? Usually, we are referring to wealth and possessions when we make this statement. Well, there have been a few folks who have tried to take some of their wealth and possessions with them. Consider the pyramids of Egypt and all of the valuables that were entombed with those of royal standing.

One more story: there was a devoutly religious father who was a member of a church that professed a strong belief in the second resurrection. That is, he believed that one day he would be physically resurrected from his own grave. Well, he had five sons. Four of the five sons went to the same church as the father. The fifth son, however, had joined a nearby Universalist church. The father was on his deathbed and he called his five sons into his room. "Sons," he said. "I don't know when the second resurrection might take place, and I don't know what things are going to be like around here when I am resurrected. But just in case there is still a need for money at that time, I'm going to ask each of you to put a hundred dollars in my casket just before I'm put into the ground." The five sons agreed.

On the day of the funeral each of the five sons walked up to the casket and one by one each son put a hundred dollar bill in an envelope taped to the inside of the casket. The Universalist son was the last to walk up to the casket. He reached into the envelope, removed the $400, and wrote a check to his dad for $500 and placed the check into the envelope.

The title of this sermon is "Beyond the Grave: Love and Immortality." And as the title implies, perhaps we don't leave everything behind at the time of our death. What if there is something that we can take with us to whatever it is that lies beyond the grave? If there is some form of life or consciousness beyond this life, wouldn't it be advisable and wise to collect whatever this material is so that we can take it with us to our next existence?

I once heard a revival sermon by a Methodist evangelist in which he described earth as a giant department store in which someone switched all the price tags before the store opened. Those items that were of the highest true value carried the cheapest prices. Those with the lowest true value carried the highest prices. We enter this life as customers entering this giant department store not knowing that the price tags have been switched.

If there were one item that you could actually take with you when you leave this life, would not that item be the most valuable of anything on earth? Perhaps our price tags have been switched. For the next twenty minutes I want to talk with you about love. I suspect love might be that priceless item that happens to carry a rather cheap price tag.

Love is central to our Universalist faith. We have often defined God as love. When I use the word *love*, I'm not using that word lightly. I've come to believe that what many of us call love is not love at all. The love of which Jesus taught is rare in our nation, rare in our churches, and rare in our families.

There are three books that I have been reading that have inspired me to write this sermon: *Anger Kills*, by Redford Williams; *Fire in the Soul*, by Joan Borysenko; and *A World Waiting to Be Born*, by Scott Peck. Add to these books some academic class work I recently completed at Duke University Medical Center in conjunction with a year of clinical pastoral education. Also, I found inspiration in rereading some of George de Benneville's rather mystical Universalist theology as well as in the rereading of some old study books from the Rosicrucian organization.

I am presently an inactive member of the Rosicrucians, but for approximately two years was a serious student of their material. I was surprised to learn at Universalist Convocation 1992 that George de Benneville had spent some time studying with the Rosicrucians. The Rosicrucian Order is a fraternal organization that traces its origin to 1300 BC in ancient Egypt. It is devoted to the teaching of metaphysical principles about life. Although I have been inactive with the Rosicrucians for several years, I continue to have a deep respect for their teachings, and I find that much of my Universalist theology is very compatible with Rosicrucian thought.

Before we look at the value of love in a possible afterlife, let's look at the value of love in this life. If there is an antithesis to human love, it must be human hostility, more commonly known as anger. In his book *Anger Kills*, the Duke psychiatrist Redford Williams gives a detailed and scientific account of the health dangers associated with hostility. I want to share with you a few brief accounts of some of his studies.

One study involved a graduating class of medical doctors from the University of North Carolina who were followed for twenty-five years after beginning their medical practice. Each of the young doctors was given psychological tests that measured their hostility level. It was found that those doctors whose hostility scores had been in the upper half of the graduating class were four to five times more likely than those with lower scores to develop coronary disease and nearly seven time more likely to die from any cause.

Another twenty-five-year study involved a selected group of male employees of Western Electric. Again, those Western Electric employees with higher hostility scores were one-and-a-half times more likely to develop coronary disease or die from any cause than were those with lower scores. It was also found in the Western Electric study that there were increased cancer deaths among the employees with the higher hostility scores.

Another study followed 118 University of North Carolina law students for twenty-five years. It was found that among those lawyers whose hostility scores had been in the highest quarter of their class twenty-five years earlier, nearly twenty percent were dead by age fifty; in contrast, only four percent of those with hostility scores in the lowest quarter had died. Another study, in Finland, found that persons who had higher hostility scores had a more than fourfold higher death rate during a follow-up period than those with lower scores.

Beyond the issue of mortality, researchers at the University of Utah found that there are harmful psychological effects from hostility. As a group, hostile people are unhappy. This study found that college students with high hostility scores report more hassles and negative life events, along with less social support. This University of Utah study also found that individuals with high levels of hostility report less marital satisfaction and more marital conflict.

Another study reported by Dr. Williams found that hostile personalities report more difficulties at work. In a study at a financial management firm of seventy-five men and women whose average age was forty, hostile individuals reported greater stress in interpersonal aspects of work, less job satisfaction, and a negative view of work relationships.

It was also found that hostile individuals tend to bring out the hostility in others with whom they interact. This, in turn, increases their anger still further, thereby making the social environment of the hostile person more stressful than that of the more loving person. Their cynical mistrust and aggressive behaviors often isolate hostile persons from sources of social support that could help to ease the harmful consequences of hostility.

Of course, no scientific study is needed to prove that most violence is due to hostility and anger. Most violent individuals are angry people.

There is proven medical value to our having loving relationships. Researchers in cardiology at Duke University recently examined the effects of social ties on survival in more than 1,300 patients who had been evaluated at Duke Medical Center in the late 1970s. Among unmarried patients who told researchers that they had no one to whom they could confide major concerns, fifty percent were dead within five years. In marked contrast, seventeen percent were dead among patients who were married, reported they had a confidant, or both. The profound impact of social isolation on survival in heart patients could not be explained by their underlying heart condition. Clearly, the lack of social ties increased the risk of dying for all patients, no matter how severe the disease.

Whether you believe in an afterlife or not, if you want this life to be a long one, you had best learn to be more loving. Anger and hostility will literally kill you. Well, I suppose what I have said so far is a sermon in itself—but let's take this notion of hostility versus love a bit further.

While completing the year of clinical pastoral education at Duke, I was exposed to a relatively new theory of personality development known as object relations theory. Basically, this theory of personality claims that our mental health and emotional wholeness is directly related to our capacity to be in relationship with others. In other words, good mental health is directly related to our capacity to love and be in loving relationships. The psychiatrist M. Scott Peck builds upon this theme in his latest book, *A World Waiting to Be Born*. He cites the classic work by the Jewish theologian Martin Buber entitled *I and Thou*. As its title indicates, Buber labeled the most healthy or mature relationship possible between two human beings as the "I-Thou" relationship. In such an instance, I recognize you to be different from me, but even though you are different—that is, a "You" or other—you can still be beloved to me, namely be a "Thou."

This really goes along with the Universalist affirmation of the divinity in all people. If we really believe in what we affirm concerning the divinity in all people, how can we relate to another human being in any manner other than I-Thou? Of course, with Universalists, as with every other religious faith and denomination, what we profess or affirm is not always what we practice. What I profess or affirm is not always what I practice. Scott Peck says that rather than have I-Thou relationships, most of us tend to have I-It relationships. In I-It relationships we lose sight of both the divinity and the humanity in the other person. Dr. Peck says that humanity's greatest sin is in not recognizing and honoring our potential for love in our relationships with one another. We tend to make "its" out of other people rather than "Thous."

Dr. Peck says that there are only two valid reasons to get married. One is for the care and upbringing of children, which is, in and of itself, a process of learning to love. The only other valid reason to get married is for the friction. Yes, friction. In fact, friction is the common denominator in any true community.

Show me a marriage in which everything is perfect and there is no friction, and I'll show you a marriage that is probably in trouble. Show me a congregation in which there is no friction, and I'll show you a congregation in which there is probably very little community. Isn't it ironic that it is out of our friction with one another that we learn to love one another?

And of course, marriage itself is an irony in learning to love. Recently, we experienced much loss following the death to cancer of a very dear member of our Red Hill Universalist Church congregation. His name was Horace Ward. Horace had been past president of the Universalist Convention of North Carolina, past moderator of the Red Hill Church, and one who often filled the pulpit when Red Hill was without a minister. I had a deep respect for Horace. He was a genuine theologian. He spent a lot of time thinking and reflecting about life, about God, and about his faith. In his coming to understand God as love, Horace drew heavily upon what he saw as the truth of procreation. He would say in so many words that we are here because of the love of our parents. In an article that he wrote for the *Universalist Herald* a few months before his death, Horace said, "We don't know whence we came, but this we know: There is no other way you could have come, except by love between a female and a male, and this is true for every living thing. This love is with you every day of life and will be with you when you go away, leading you on into the great unknown." Horace was also saying that love may be something you could take with you, wasn't he? I think Horace was also alluding to that which is now known as the object relations theory of personality development.

I think we need to differentiate between lust and love. However, let's not put lust in a negative light. Sexual attraction is a beautiful and powerful aspect of creation. Sexual attraction is one of the factors that bring human beings together. Yet we must remember that sexual attraction is not love. Many folks may marry for lust, but if they stay together beyond a couple of years, it is usually because of their ability in learning to love.

Object relations theory holds that we are all born as very narcissistic. That is, children tend to be very selfish and self-centered. As we grow into adulthood, the healthy individuals evolve from being selfish and self-centered into becoming giving and loving. Object relations theory holds that most teenagers and young adults who "fall in love" are actually falling for their own narcissistic fantasies of the other person. It is not so much love as it is narcissism coupled with sexual attraction that we call "falling in love." But that's OK because that is how it appears human nature was created. If it were not for this illusion of falling madly in love, most folks would never get together in the first place. Sigmund Freud considered romantic love as temporary insanity. Love is what happens after romantic intoxication has subsided. Love is born out of our friction with one another. Love is born out of our working at a relationship with another person.

As Horace Ward observed, isn't it amazing how Mother Nature or God appears to have created us in a manner in which we are almost forced to learn to love one another?

Yes, sexual attraction is one factor that brings us together in relationship, but perhaps the fear of loneliness is an equal force that brings us together. Psychologists tell us that our greatest fear is isolation and loneliness. Individuals who are isolated from other human beings for an extended period of time literally go crazy. The human being cannot live in total isolation and remain sane.

Are you beginning to grasp what I am trying to say in this morning's sermon? If there is any apparent divine plan or divine purpose to human life, it would appear that such a plan or purpose is related to our need to learn to love one another. Might it be that we are here for only that purpose? Is that not what Jesus of Nazareth was trying to teach us in telling us to love one another, and in teaching us to do unto others as you would have them do unto you, and in proclaiming that we should love one another as we love ourselves? I'm suggesting that the teaching to love one another goes beyond good ethical living. Perhaps love is more than just a good idea for human relations. What if love and learning to love is the whole purpose of human existence?

But we have more than medical studies, psychological theories, theological commentaries, and the teaching of Jesus to hint that learning to love is what human life is all about. Joan Borysenko, a Harvard-trained PhD psychologist, has written a fascinating book entitled *Fire in the Soul*, which delves into spirituality, psychology, and metaphysics to understand the meaning of love. Dr. Borysenko has come to believe in the existence of a human soul. I, too, have come to believe in the existence of the human soul. It baffles me when I hear from many modern Unitarian Universalist humanists that belief in the existence of the human soul is an antiquated and unscientific concept. From what reading I have done in the area of quantum physics, it seems that modern science is much more receptive to the idea of a spiritual realm of existence and the possibility of the human soul than at any time in the past century. And let us not forget that the beginnings of Universalism were grounded in a belief in the human soul and in the belief of immortality for that human soul.

In her book, Dr. Borysenko recounts numerous near-death experiences in which individuals recalled conscious memories of their near-death experiences. What is fascinating was how similar the accounts are! There tended to be a universal experience of being pulled toward a brilliant white light, and as the individual or soul came closer to that light, there was an immense feeling of love, an experience of love beyond anything ever known before. Individuals revived after such experiences often expressed abrupt changes in their beliefs about life and God. Despite the tragedies and trials of life, they tended to affirm the belief that they are safe in a universe that is ultimately loving. This experience of encountering a loving presence in the form of a brilliant light has happened so many times in near-death experiences that it is now taught to many medical students as a part of their course curriculum in dealing with death and dying. I know for a fact that it is now taught at the medical schools at Duke and at the University of North Carolina.

But let's go back to the book *Fire in the Soul*. I want to read to you one of Dr. Borysenko's numerous accounts: one of a woman named Donna whose heart stopped beating during surgery. Donna described leaving her body, looking down at the operating room scene, hearing the medical staff yelling they'd "lost her" and then floating off into a "bold, bright, white light." She then moved through a tunnel that she described in great detail, feeling peaceful, calmer, and more loving as she ascended through it. Under hypnosis, Donna told about her experience:

> I am slowly, slowly floating and floating. I love, love, love. I love myself. I am filled with love. I am experiencing affection on an immeasurable level. This affection and love is sent to me and is coming from me to me at me at the same time. The affection I feel in me is for everything, not just myself. I understand this. . . . I feel the deepest feeling of acceptance. I am loved. It is beautiful here. It is so peaceful. It is so tranquil. . . . The weight of life is lifted off my shoulders.

Dr. Borysenko tells of many other such incidents. She found that when such people as Donna return to their bodies, the overwhelming majority believe that the most important thing in life is love.

As I read these accounts, I couldn't help but think of the parallel with the story of Universalism's own George de Benneville, who came to embrace the Universalist idea of God as love following his own near-death experience. You might recall that de Benneville was assumed dead and had been already placed in his coffin when he was somehow revived from his unconsciousness. Later, de Benneville claimed a very vivid memory of his near-death experience, quite similar to that of others. He claimed to have encountered spiritual guides as well as a great white light that he understood to be God. It was while in the proximity of this divine light that de Benneville felt and understood love with richness and depth he had never known before. This near-death experience was pivotal in de Benneville's strong faith in God as love and the importance of learning to love one another during this lifetime.

Life is such a mystery, isn't it? We pretend to know so much, but in reality we know practically nothing.

What if love is a substance? What if love is the only substance? But what if part of the dilemma of being human is that we are unable to see love for what it is? More precious than gold, more precious than diamonds, yet it carries such a cheap price tag. Paul writes in 1 Corinthians 13:

> Now all we can see of God is like a cloudy picture in a mirror. Later we will see him face to face. We don't know everything, but then we will, just as God completely understands us. For now there are faith, hope, and love. But of these three, the greatest is love. (1 Cor 13: 12–13)

Faith, hope, and love are all three invisible and immeasurable spiritual qualities. Perhaps at death we are visibly able to see all three. But if there is only one of these three qualities that will go with us to whatever lives beyond the grave, I suggest to you that it will be love.

Maybe you can take it with you!

Delivered during Sunday morning worship service, September 18, 1994, Universalist Convocation 1994, Westfield Center Universalist Church, Westfield Center, Ohio.

2

Light and Darkness

DARKNESS AND LIGHT ARE the two principal metaphors of the Bible. They appear right off in the opening words of Genesis: "The earth was barren with no form of life; it was under a roaring ocean covered with darkness. But the Spirit of God was moving over the water. God said, 'I command light to shine!' And light started shining. God looked at the light and saw that it was good. He separated light from darkness" (Gen 1:2–4).

The Gospel of John is filled with references to light and darkness. In the first chapter of John it is written:

> In the beginning was the one who is called the Word. The Word was with God and was truly God. From the very beginning the Word was with God. And with this Word, God created all things. Nothing was made without the Word. Everything that was created received its life from him, and his life gave light to everyone. The light keeps shining in the dark, and darkness has never put it out. God sent a man named John, who came to tell about the light and to lead all people to have faith. John wasn't that light. He came only to tell about the light. (John 1:1–8)

And from Isaiah 9 we find references to light and darkness in the passage of scripture often read during the Christmas season, "Those who walked in the dark have seen a bright light. And it shines upon everyone who lives in the land of darkest shadows" (Isa 9:2).

The Christmas season is a time when lights are most prominently used in celebration. No other holiday—no other time of the year—do we celebrate with lights as we do at Christmas: candlelight services, Christmas tree lights, electric candle lights in windows, colorful lights adorning main streets in every town and city, lighted Santa Clauses, strings of lights wrapped around front porches and outside trees.

What is the meaning of our Christmas lights? Is our December celebration of lights merely a custom that has no meaning beyond that of tradition, or might there be a deeper meaning in our Christmas lights?

According to a Roman almanac, the Christian festival of Christmas was celebrated in Rome by AD 336. The traditional customs connected with Christmas have developed from several sources as a result of the coincidence of the celebration of the birth of Jesus with the pagan agricultural and solar observances at midwinter. In the Roman world, December 17 was a time of merrymaking and exchange of gifts. December 25 was also regarded as the birth date of the Iranian mystery god Mithra, the Sun of Righteousness. In the Jewish tradition, December 20 marks the beginning of Hanukkah. It is a festival of lights commemorating the victory of the Maccabees over Antiochus of Syria and their rededication of the defiled temple of Israel. On the Roman New Year (January 1), houses were decorated with greenery and lights, and gifts were given to children and the poor. To these observances were added the German and Celtic winter Yule rites of food and good fellowship, the Yule log and Yule cakes. However, in all of these different winter traditions, fire and lights have been an integral part of the celebration. What is the meaning of our December lights?

December 21 is the day of the winter solstice. For those of us living in the Northern Hemisphere, December 21 is the day of greatest darkness. We have less sunlight on December 21 than at any other time of the year. Is it our collective fear of darkness that brings forth our December lights?

There is the story of a trip made by a father and his two-and-a-half-year-old son. It was the first time the father and the boy had been away by themselves—just the two of them. The first night they spent in a hotel, the father moved his bed close to the little boy's, and when they were both tucked in, he turned out the light.

After a few minutes, a little voice said: "It sure is dark, isn't it?"

"Yes," said the father, "it's pretty dark, but everything is all right."

There was silence for a few more minutes, and then a little hand reached over and took the father's hand. "I'll just hold your hand," said the little boy, "in case you get scared."

In a book by Thomas Butts entitled *Tigers in the Dark*, the author tells about a time when all the electricity went out at a Barnum and Bailey Circus. For a few minutes they were all in total darkness. They had just started the act with the tigers in the cage with the trainer. When the lights came on the trainer was still alive. He was interviewed by television and newspaper reporters and was asked: "How did you feel in that cage with all those big tigers in the dark . . . when they could see you and you couldn't see them?" The tiger trainer's answer was this: "But they didn't know I couldn't see them . . . so I just cracked my whip and shouted commands."

Perhaps our displaying of Christmas lights is somewhat similar to the trainer cracking his whip and shouting commands. It is our way of pretending that this season is not as dark as it actually is. Do our Christmas lights help alleviate our fear of darkness?

Beyond the fear of darkness, our attraction to Christmas lights might also indicate both a physical and an emotional need. It was discovered in 1967 that Vitamin D is manufactured by the skin only in the presence of sunlight. A deficiency of Vitamin D will result in the bone-deforming disease known as rickets. Today we usually get adequate Vitamin D regardless of our exposure to sunlight because of the supplemental Vitamin D that we get from vitamin pills and irradiated milk. But thirty years ago this was not the case. And it was in the winter when the sun's rays were most feeble and children were bundled up in layers of clothing that rickets most often attacked its victims.

However, more recent studies have found that sunlight also affects our emotional health. Researchers have found that sunlight deprivation results in mild to severe depression in many people. Some studies indicate that as many as one in every three persons experience some degree of depression from sunlight deprivation. One treatment for this type of depression involves exposure to an ultraviolet light, such as a sunlamp, for twenty minutes a day. Might our attraction to and use of Christmas lights be related to both physical and emotional health needs?

Darkness, in scripture, is something bad, something to get away from. Light, on the other hand, is something good, something to walk toward. Evil is darkness; God is light. Sin is moral darkness; the gospel is light. This dichotomy appears over and over in the Bible. As a metaphor we speak of the darkness of evil, the darkness of ignorance, the darkness of tragic suffering, the darkness of terror and tragedy, and the darkness of despair and depression. Likewise, we metaphorically use light in describing good, such as the light of righteousness, the light of wisdom, the light of hope, the light of understanding, and the light of love. In the Christian religion, Christ has been called the light of the world.

In our Universalist tradition, John Murray made use of light in a metaphorical way when he said, "Remember, you possess only a small light, but uncover it, let it shine, use it in order to bring more light and understanding to the hearts and minds of men and women. Give them, not hell, but hope and courage." And it was Jesus who said, "I am the light of the world," and he said to his disciples, "You are the light of the world; let your light shine."

According to a study by Edgar Jackson, in the average parish congregation there is much metaphorical darkness. His study indicates that one-fifth of a congregation will be feeling a sense of darkness because of a recent death. A third of the congregation will be facing the darkness of divorce, marital difficulty, or problems in a dating relationship. About half of the congregation will be having dark problems adjusting emotionally to school, job, home, or community. A few others will be afflicted with a deep sense of guilt and shame stemming from aspects of their behavior.

Might our attraction to and use of Christmas lights be a metaphorical statement? Might our December lights be symbols of goodness, symbols of righteousness, symbols of healing, symbols of forgiveness, symbols of wisdom, symbols of hope, symbols of understanding, and symbols of love for those in our midst who are experiencing metaphorical spiritual darkness?

Might it be possible that our attraction to Christmas lights indicate something much deeper? Perhaps the biblical use of light and darkness is more than metaphorical? In Ephesians 5, Paul makes a special point that Christians are those who have transferred from the realm of darkness to the realm of light. I would like to think we could broaden Paul's use of *Christian* to include all individuals who are embarked on an intentional faith journey. Paul says in effect that "if you are in the light and the light is in you, you should walk in the light and have done with the deeds of darkness." And then in verse 14 Paul writes that "Christ shall give you light." Again, I wish to interpret the term *Christ* in a universal manner, that is, Christ as indwelling God, the indwelling God of all religious paths.

Might spiritual references to light and darkness have more than metaphorical meaning? What if there is some literal meaning to the spiritual references to light and darkness? We know from science that the human eye is limited in what it can see as visible. Take for example infrared light. Unless we are looking through a special lens that allows us to see infrared light, infrared light is invisible. Yet, with an infrared seeing device, a human being is clearly visible despite apparent darkness. I give this illustration to demonstrate that light and darkness as applied to human life can have literal meaning. Might there be a spiritual range of light and darkness, similar to infrared light, that most human beings are unable to see? Might our attraction to Christmas lights be indicative of a deeper yearning, a yearning for spiritual light?

The history of the Christian church includes several different mystical schools of thought known as Gnosticism. In fact, aspects of early Universalist philosophy are rooted in Gnosticism. A characteristic doctrine running through all the different varieties of Christian Gnosticism was that the impersonal and unknowable God, the ground of our being, existed in the form of pure light.

Gnosticism is now considered a heresy, but how do you explain the orthodox account of Saul's conversion as recorded in the ninth chapter of Acts? In verse 3 it is written, "Suddenly, while he was traveling to Damascus and just before he reached the city, there came a light from heaven all around him." This reference to light in Acts 9 is not metaphorical. According to Saul, who later changed his name to Paul, it was a very real light that surrounded him, and almost blinded him, during his trip to Damascus.

I also find it interesting that in many of the accounts of near-death experiences, individuals tell of encountering or being drawn toward a bright light. In *Guilt Is the Teacher, Love Is the Lesson*, Joan Borysenko tells several stories of patients, colleagues, and friends who had visions, near-death experiences, and meetings with a radiant light through which they directly apprehended higher levels of meaning, found physical and/ or psychological healing, and came to believe that despite the tragedies and trials of life they were safe in a universe that was ultimately loving.

These accounts are similar to that of our own George de Benneville, eighteenth-century Universalist mystic and preacher, who was further convinced of Universalism following his own near-death experience. In recalling his vision of light during his near-death experience, de Benneville wrote, "it was the fire of heavenly love, filled with light as with rays of the sun."

Consider the following incident that was reported in the May 1971 *Canadian Medical Association Journal*. According to the physicians who wrote the article, this particular patient had suffered a cardiac arrest while a patient in the cardiac unit at Toronto General Hospital. Since he was on a heart monitor, the nurses on the unit immediately saw that his heart had stopped beating and they quickly went to work to revive the man. Once this patient regained consciousness, he relayed a very vivid memory of the events surrounding his near-death experience. I only want to share with you what he had to say about light:

> Down below to my left I saw a pure white cloud-like substance also moving up on the line that would intersect my course. Somehow I was able to go down and take a look at it. Two thoughts came to me: "What will happen to me when it engulfs me?" and "You don't have to worry; it has all happened before and everything will be taken care of." My next sensation was of floating in a bright, pale yellow light—a very delightful feeling. I continued to float, enjoying the most beautiful tranquil sensation. I had never experienced such a delightful sensation and have no words to describe it.

Another near-death experience is told by Julia Phillips Ruopp and is written in Jess Weiss's *The Vestibule*. Again, I will limit the story to that which deals with light. She writes:

> I started through what seemed to be a long, dark passageway, and as I went along I thought calmly, "This must be what they call dying." This journey continued uneventful for some time, and I was beginning to wonder how long it would last, when I emerged into an overwhelmingly wide space of light—a pulsing, living light which cannot be described in words. Here my body felt light and free and for a little while drifted about with no apparent destination.

There are literally hundreds of other written accounts of near-death experiences in which individuals claim to have experienced an encounter with something spectacular that they describe as light. So common are the reports of experiencing a brilliant light at the time of death that some medical schools now include this phenomenon in their courses concerning death and dying.

A personal experience of my own involving light that I cannot explain occurred during a period in my life in which I was very involved with meditation. I had read that individuals sometimes experienced the sensation of a light during meditation, but I had taken this to be either metaphorical or the product of a vivid imagination. But one evening as I meditated in a darkened room, I was startled to suddenly see a yellow glow of light against my closed eyelids. I immediately thought that someone was shining a flashlight into the room from the nearby window. I quickly opened my eyes, but there was no flashlight or any other light in the room. I closed my eyes and returned to my meditation. Again, the light appeared. Again, I opened my eyes. Again, there was no explanation for the light. I then wondered: could this be the light that is sometimes experienced in meditation? I went into my hallway, closing the doors behind me. Now there was no possible way that light from a window could reach my closed eyelids. A few minutes back into my meditation, the yellow glow of light once again appeared against my closed eyelids. With much excitement, I arose and telephoned two good friends who had had more experience with meditation than I to tell them what had happened. I found that they had had such experiences as well. Over the course of the next several months, there were many other occasions in which I experienced this same light during my meditations.

Several years later while pursuing doctoral studies in the area of Christian spirituality, I learned that early Christian mystics and spiritual teachers also experienced lights during their prayer. John of the Cross, who lived in the 1500s, called this phenomenon "locutions." He taught his disciples that this was a normal occurrence that many individuals experienced after committing to a spiritual discipline. He warned against paying much attention to this visual phenomenon because in putting importance on these lights one can easily become distracted from one's spiritual path and from God. He taught that it was not the light that was important, but rather it was the quality of our love.

Christmas lights! What is it that attracts us to the lights of December? Tradition? Fear of darkness? Physical health? Emotional health? Metaphorical spiritual meaning? Or might there be some literal spiritual meaning surrounding light and darkness? Might spiritual light and divine love be one and the same? Might our attraction to Christmas lights be indicative of a much deeper spiritual yearning? I don't have the answer. I leave you with the question. What is it that attracts you to the lights of Christmas?

3

What Is Universalism?

MANY TIMES UNIVERSALISTS ARE asked to explain the meaning of our liberal religious faith. The question is asked, What is Universalism? A couple of years ago I was visiting in my hometown of Waterloo, South Carolina, and the father of a classmate friend of mine during elementary and junior high school came into the store. After a few minutes of visiting and catching-up on one another's families, the topic turned to what I was now doing to make a living. And after I mentioned the term *Universalist*, my friend's father was quick to respond, "Oh yeah, I've heard of your church—that's the one headed by that Moon fellow in Korea!" I went on to explain that Universalism has no relation to Unification.

My immediate family members are life-long Methodists, and my ninety-eight-year-old grandmother, Myrtis "Nanny" Broome, whom I love dearly, occasionally will ask me to explain to her the difference between Universalists and the Methodists. The first time she asked me that question, I responded with a rather lengthy—maybe five-minute—but delicate overview of the history and theology of both Unitarianism and Universalism. I had hoped to explain to her the differences between how a Methodist and a Universalist might believe concerning God, Jesus, the Bible, and salvation, but I did not want to shock her with my explanation. After I had finished talking there was a period of silence. I broke the silence by asking my grandmother, "Well, Nanny, what do you think about my church?"

My grandmother responded, "Well, it sounds like a good church to me. It really doesn't matter what church we go to anyway as long as you believe in Jesus as our Savior and believe the Bible."

I've yet to decide if I was too delicate in my explanation or if my grandmother heard only what she wanted to hear!

Our larger denomination is known as the Unitarian Universalist Association. I used to tell folks that the Unitarian Universalist Association was the result of a merger between the Unitarians and the Universalists in 1961. My colleague Al Niles, with fifty years experience in the Universalist ministry, has since educated me to the fact that there never was any merger. It was a formal consolidation. This new association was more akin to a marriage than it was to the creation of a new denomination.

When I first united with this religious denomination back in 1975, I considered myself, first and foremost, a Unitarian Universalist. I was particularly attracted to the freedom that this church allowed its members. As I read both Unitarian and Universalist history, I was proud of both religious traditions—and I am still proud of both the Unitarian and Universalist traditions. I was ordained by one of the largest Unitarian Universalist congregations in the United States: the Unitarian Universalist Congregation of Atlanta, Georgia. It was also with this congregation that I spent a one-semester student internship in 1976.

However, over the past eight years, I have increasingly found more spiritual comfort in those congregations that have retained a Universalist character, and my evolving theology has felt more compatible with historical Universalism. Gradually, I have come to simply call myself a "Universalist." One reason that I do this is as a reaction to those within the Unitarian Universalist Association who only use the word "Unitarian" in identifying their faith. Also, the term "UU" has come to have a superficial connotation. It seems in reducing Unitarian Universalism to the two letters UU, we remove the rich heritages of both Unitarianism and Universalism. Lastly, I choose to now call myself a "Universalist" because the term "Universalist" identifies my religious place and religious heritage within the very broad spectrum of what constitutes Unitarian Universalism today.

What is Universalism? Historically, the term "Universalism" usually refers to the doctrine or philosophy that ultimately all persons will be saved from sin and misery. By this I mean a rejection of the notion of an everlasting hell in an afterlife. A secondary meaning of the term "Universalism" refers to the notion of a divine element or principle common to all natural phenomena. Now both of these definitions of "Universalism" have been found in various philosophies and teachings in various cultures and religions since before the origin of Christianity.

In early Christianity, various Christian groups embraced aspects of a "Universalist" philosophy. The early Christian theologians Clement of Alexandria and Origen both embraced the doctrine of universal salvation. It was not until AD 544 that Universalism was officially labeled a heresy by the Catholic Church.

What is Universalism? My previous discussion concerned the philosophy of Universalism. Let's take a look at how Universalism becomes an organized religious faith. Although Universalism has been considered a heresy by the Christian church since AD 544, there have continued to be various individuals who, nonetheless, embraced a Universalist philosophy. In the 1700s it was among the Methodists in England that the heresy of Universalism occasionally found expression. And when an English Methodist minister was found to be preaching Universalism, his preaching credentials were quickly withdrawn. And here we find the beginnings of the Universalist Church. There was a James Relly, who had been converted to Methodism by the Methodist evangelist George Whitfield. Relly worked with Whitfield for a number of years until he and Whitfield disagreed over the issue of universal salvation. Relly left the Methodist church but continued his own brand of Universalism until his death in 1778 at the age of fifty-six. He also wrote a book entitled *Union*. Remember this book, *Union*; you will hear about it again.

Now there was another Englishman, John Murray, born in 1741, reared in the Calvinist religion, who as a young man attained a license to preach in the Methodist Church. As a young Methodist preacher, Murray hated those who embraced Universalism. However, after coming across and reading a copy of Relly's book *Union*, Murray began to have some ambivalent feelings about his orthodox faith. In 1757, Murray attended his first service led by James Relly, and by 1760 he had become a complete convert to what was then known as Rellyism. Of course, he was shortly thereafter voted out of his Methodist society.

After being asked to leave the Methodist Church, several other tragedies came to bear on John Murray. Although history does not record the details, Murray was arrested for debt, which he somehow managed to pay after his arrest. Later he experienced the death of his only son at the age of one. His wife's health began to decline and she later died. Within this same five-year period, Murray lost a brother and three sisters. Depression and loneliness plagued Murray. He often thought of suicide. It was only his relationship with James Relly that seemed to sustain him. Relly continually urged Murray to be a spokesman for Universalism, but Murray no longer had any interest in preaching. He heard stories about the new world of America. He yearned to leave England and all his sad memories and live out the remainder of his years in obscurity in the wilderness of America.

John Murray's decision to come to America was an essentially negative one—to avoid further misery rather than to seek happiness. On a Saturday evening, July 21, 1770, he sailed from England on board the brig *Hand-in-Hand*, with a little money, some clothes, a Bible, a bundle of his late wife's letters, and various other papers.

On the other side of the Atlantic was a colorful character, considered a little crazy by his neighbors, by the name of Thomas Potter. Potter was not an educated man, but he was deeply religious with an attraction to mysticism. Potter had made a small fortune from the lumber business and had used some of his earnings to build a meeting house for itinerant or traveling preachers to use. He had been reared as a Baptist, but had somehow come across a copy of Relly's book *Union*. In building his meeting house, Potter genuinely believed that God would eventually send him a preacher who preached Universalism.

Murray's ship was to have sailed to New York, but by mistake the captain sailed to Philadelphia. From Philadelphia the ship set sail for New York but it became grounded on a sandbar off Cranberry Inlet in Barnegat Bay on the southern coast of New Jersey. This just happened to be where Thomas Potter lived and where he had built his meeting house. While the ship was grounded, Murray went ashore with others to seek provisions. Murray met Potter and there was sufficient conversation for Potter to learn that Murray embraced a Universalist theology. Potter begged Murray to preach. Murray refused. Murray said that he intended to leave for New York just as soon as the wind changed, allowing the ship to sail from the sandbar. Finally Potter told Murray, "The wind will never change, sir, until you have delivered to us, in that meeting house, a message from God." Three days later the wind had still not changed, and Murray consented to preach in Potter's meeting house. And he continued preaching. In 1779 he formed the first Universalist church.

Murray's church was the first organized Universalist church in America, but Universalism as an idea had been popping up a lot in America. Some who advocated it later became a part of this new denomination. One such preacher was Elhanan Winchester, a Baptist preacher whose first pastorate was near the Great Pee Dee River in South Carolina, about ninety miles southwest of the Red Hill Universalist Church in North Carolina. There he shocked his parish and shortened his tenure by teaching the slaves and even inviting them to church. Winchester moved to Philadelphia, where he met another preacher/physician who had been preaching a mystical Universalism for several years in Pennsylvania. This man's name was George de Benneville. De Benneville embraced a mystical Universalist theology following an incident years earlier when he had been mistakenly taken for dead when in fact he was in a deep coma. After he had been placed in his coffin de Benneville awoke from his coma and startled his mourners by climbing out of the coffin. De Benneville had vivid memories of his three days in the coma, and for him this near-death experience was a religious revelation. What he later wrote describing this unusual experience is quite similar to the out-of-body experiences collected by Elizabeth Kubler-Ross in recent times. At any rate, all three of these men, Murray, Winchester, and de Benneville eventually met and became spokesmen for the newly formed Universalist Church in America.

But it was Hosea Ballou, born the year after Murray preached his first sermon in Potter's meeting house, who was to be the theological giant of the denomination. His mature thought produced a remarkable document, *A Treatise on Atonement*, a synthesis of Ballou's personal pietism and the Deism of the enlightenment that he found expressed by many around him. Not only did Ballou embrace the notion of universal salvation, but he also preached Unitarianism, the doctrine that God is one rather than a trinity. In his treatise, Ballou outlined the old theory of atonement as preached by the orthodox Christians, which stated that humanity's sins against God were so infinite and deserved a punishment so great that no mere human could take it on. So, God himself, in the form of Jesus Christ, took on the punishment for all of humanity by dying on the cross. "Nonsense," said Ballou. "No loving God would be so bloodthirsty and vengeful. Humans sin, all right, but their sins make them miserable right here on earth, and a loving God is engaged always in trying to win us back to goodness and happiness. The saving act of Jesus," said Ballou "is in his showing us a moral and beauty-filled way to live, which will allow us to be happy. Jesus' life and message, not his death, are the good news of Universalism. There is no need to assume that Jesus is God," said Ballou. "Jesus was a special human being sent by God, endowed with the Truth of God. But Jesus was not God."

Ballou's view of Jesus became an important tenet of Universalism. Universalists began to call their faith the "religion of Jesus rather than the religion about Jesus." Universalists did not reject the divinity in Jesus, but rather they rejected making Jesus a deity.

Although Universalists were preaching a Universalism that was theologically Unitarian by 1800, the Unitarians by and large had no interest in the Universalists. It would not be until the 1900s that the American Unitarian Association would show any interest in uniting with the Universalists. The differences were not so much theological as social. Many of the upper-crust Bostonians of the Unitarian Church wanted nothing to do with ex-Baptists from the Carolina and Georgia backwoods. This Unitarian attitude lent credence to the often repeated comment that "the difference between Unitarians and Universalists was that Universalists believe that God is too good to damn them to hell, and the Unitarians believe that they are too good to be damned to hell." And it was further said, "Unitarians believed in the Fatherhood of God, the Brotherhood of Jesus, and the Neighborhood of Boston, while the Universalists struck out for the south, the mill towns, and the frontier."

Universalists were further agreed on the importance of this life and the importance of good social conditions conducive to morality and happiness. They founded many schools, including Tufts University, University of Akron, St. Lawrence School of Theology, and the California Institute of Technology. They took an active part in the early women's movement, were the first body to ordain a woman to the ministry, and perhaps more remarkable, settled a number of women ministers in parishes between 1863 and the First World War. The early Universalists were quite active in prohibition, temperance, and the social gospel movements. And, in general, they worked out their belief that happiness and productivity for all people in this life are important religious concerns. Near the turn of the century, the Universalist Church of American was the sixth largest denomination in this country.

The decline of the Universalist denomination in the 1900s has been attributed to several reasons: (1) Many mainline Christian denominations became less focused on hell-fire theology and gradually adopted some of the Universalist ideas. (2) The Universalists have never taught that their faith was the only valid spiritual path. In respecting religious diversity, Universalists have never sought to convert others to their way of belief.

And (3) Universalists lacked the denominational organization that other mainline churches were able to develop.

But what is Universalism today? Universalism is a liberal religious faith with much to offer modern America. Central to the Universalist faith is the principle of the free mind. Paraphrasing the words of John Nichols Booth, the Universalist Church insists that intellectual honesty, moral progress, and spiritual growth in religion are dependent upon each person being receptive to all pronouncements of truth, wherever and by whomever uttered. Our roots are in the Judeo-Christian heritage, but we recognize that truth is universal. The Universalist sees truth in all religions.

The principle of the free mind means that as Universalists our faith does not have to be anti-scientific or overly scientific, but that it can be co-scientific. The principle of the free mind means that our Universalist faith can be an exciting and adventurous life-long journey of discovery instead of stagnating with creeds and doctrines that do not make sense. The principle of the free mind means that for Universalists revelation has not ceased, and that there is new religious truth to be discovered in the heart of each of us.

What is Universalism today? It is the belief in the dignity of human nature. We affirm that the human experience with its glory and suffering, joy and sorrow, ecstasy and despair is, nonetheless, good and worthwhile. Universalists believe in the dignity of every human being and we applaud efforts to help people grow in a sense of self-respect.

What is Universalism today? We are a faith that treasures the Judeo-Christian Bible as a precious collection of spiritual truths and insights, but we do not accept this, or any other "holy" book, as the infallible or exclusive word of God. We can appreciate the Bible without making the Bible a deity to worship.

What is Universalism today? Ours is a faith that helps us foster a mature and genuine understanding of love. In our modern times, many in American society have come to regard love as a commodity. Universalism stresses values and goals that foster mature love. We encourage people to trust each other, to accept other people, and to accept themselves. We believe that mature love is based on cooperation and respect for the integrity of the other person and not on manipulation and exploitation. The mature love that Universalism nourishes is based on a willingness to take risks with people, to reach out and touch the mystery of another human being. In a society that has come to worship the idea of independence, the mature love fostered by our faith stresses interdependence and community.

What is Universalism today? Ours is a faith that teaches tolerance. A colleague of mine recently made the joke that UUs practice tolerance for all groups and beliefs except Christians, Republicans, the U.S. military, and pro-life advocates. Many UUs laugh at this statement because there is truth in this humor. And that's sad! The tolerance of Universalism includes not just tolerance, but acceptance of those in our congregations who may identify as Christians, Republicans, members of the U.S. Armed Forces and/or pro-lifers. The Universalist symbol of the cross and offsetting circle signify this tolerance. Whereas other churches drew creedal circles that shut people out, Universalists drew a circle that took folks in.

What is Universalism today? We can be a liberal religious faith and yet still be comfortable with the use of religious language. This is not always the case with some UU and Unitarian groups. Religious words such as God, sin, prayer, spirituality, guilt, forgiveness—these words have meaning for most Universalists. Our understanding of these terms may take on a more liberal or freer meaning than that of our Baptist neighbors, but nonetheless, much traditional religious language has relevance for Universalists.

What is Universalism today? Universalists believe in the importance of social action, but our call to social action is a byproduct of our faith. For Universalists, social action alone does not meet the criteria for being religious. Here we also differ from some of our UU and Unitarian brothers and sisters. For Universalists, social action is the practical application of our belief in the doctrine of love. And as Universalists, we recognize that there will be differences among us in how we interpret our call to social action.

What is Universalism today? Ours is a liberal religious community rooted in the Judeo-Christian tradition that is based on freedom, responsibility, human dignity, mature love, and an openness to experience that which we call God in our relationships with one another and with our world. Ours is a faith that challenges us and demands the best that we can give. Ultimately, each one of us is engaged in a solitary and personal religious pilgrimage, but we give depth and form and meaning to our solitary destinies through our association with others. Universalism is a liberal religious community in which we try to humanize this life, in which we build bonds of caring and compassion and discover that bit of heaven in each person. Universalism, at its best, is a community that helps us find God in the smile of a child, the warm touch of a hand, and in the words of love we speak to one another.

Delivered on September 21, 1991, Universalist Convocation 1991, Potter's Chapel, Murray Grove, New Jersey. Note: My maternal grandmother, Myrtis Beatrice Spires Broome, who is mentioned at the beginning of this sermon, died on December 24, 1991.

4

Universalism: A Remedy
for Homesick Religious Liberals

2 Corinthians 4:1–3, 7–9, 13

HOME! THINK ON THAT word for a moment! Do you realize how important a sense of home is in your life?

Along with my parish ministry to the Outlaw's Bridge and Red Hill congregations, I am presently involved with a one-year clinical pastoral education program at nearby Duke University Medical Center. About half of my time at the hospital is spent visiting patients on the several units to which I am assigned. Of the many concerns or requests for prayer that I have heard while standing or sitting in patient rooms, I have been impressed with how many times the word *home* comes up in my pastoral conversations. Folks who are confined to hospital rooms want to get well so that they can return home! For the past several weeks I have made regular visits to one seventeen-year-old boy who was injured in a shooting incident. The bullet passed through his left lung and slightly punctured a valve in his heart. The first night following surgery it was not known whether this teenage boy would live or die. However, his body has shown a miraculous ability to heal. Within a couple of days the heart tissue began to heal itself without the need of additional surgery. The boy will eventually recover. However on every occasion that I have visited this patient, his request of me has been the same: "Chaplain, will you please say a prayer for me that I will soon be able to return home?"

Today he is slated to be released from the hospital after a thirty-three-day stay, and I assume he is now back at home.

I have also witnessed the behavior of patients who are not so fortunate as to return home. A thirty-year-old Cherokee Indian from the western part of North Carolina was hospitalized this past August with an incurable liver disease. He, too, requested me to say prayers that he might be able to return home. However, with every passing week, his condition worsened. As it became more obvious that this young man might never return to his home in the Blue Ridge Mountains, his bedside stand and the walls of his room became covered with pictures and photographs suggesting memories of his home and of his people. A week ago last Tuesday he died in his hospital room.

Perhaps needing a sense of home is not limited to human creatures. We know that many species of migratory birds return to the same vicinity of the nests from which they were hatched. We can observe this same "homecoming" among various species of fish and reptiles. Some might argue that this behavior in birds, fish, and reptiles is not a yearning for home as much as it is instinct related to the creature's reproductive cycle. Maybe so! But how do you explain the numerous stories of pets that have been known to travel hundreds of miles to return to places that they know as home?

A few years ago in Geneva, Florida, a seven-hundred-pound cow, soon to have a calf, was sold to a cattle rancher who lived thirty-five miles from the farm where this cow was raised. The cow obviously was not happy with the arrangement, for twenty-four hours later she was back home—about one hundred pounds lighter and covered with scratches. Her curious owner tracked the cow and found she had jumped out of her pen, leaped over two barbed wire fences, forded a river, crossed highways, and ignored a driving rain in her determined cross-country trip.

Home! Perhaps our yearning for that which we call home or think as home is a much greater force in our consciousness than we ever imagined. And when we are far away from that which is home—and are unable to create or form a new sense of home—perhaps the experience of homesickness is a much more serious illness than we oftentimes think of it being.

In the heart of every person there is an awful homesickness for wholeness, for relatedness, for unity. All through our lives, one of our deepest needs is to overcome our separateness. It could be said that the absolute failure to achieve this aim means insanity.

Modern America is a people yearning for home. Modern America is a homesick nation, and our homesickness is manifested in our alienation, distrust, and fear of one another.

We religious liberals are not immune from this cultural homesickness. We too suffer the pain of alienation, distrust, and fear.

We are a nation yearning for home. We are a nation yearning for love. We are a nation yearning for God. But in the words of the recently popular country music song, "we're looking for love in all the wrong places." What are the false homesick remedies in America today? I term these false homesick remedies as "the idolatry of materialism," "the idolatry of liberty," and "the idolatry of individualism."

The lie of materialism would have us believe that the sense of home is found in the acquisition, accumulation, and ownership of *things*. *The idolatry of materialism is a form of homesickness.*

The lie of the idolatry of liberty is that it negates responsibility. There should be a sister statue to the Statue of Liberty in New York City harbor: the "Statue of Responsibility." Liberty is a wonderful value, but only as it is bridled with responsibility. Liberty without responsibility is a cancer within a community. Such liberty breeds narcissism and decadence. *The idolatry of liberty is a form of homesickness.*

And the lie of modern American individualism is that one does not need community. The healthy individualism that characterized early America was one in which individuals were independent but were also mutually supportive and caring neighbors. Community was expressed by concern for the common good and civic virtue. Modern American individualism values self-expression and idealizes the form of social life that places minimal restraints on the individual pursuit of money, goods, and power. Modern American individualism lacks a vision and concern for the common good. *The idolatry of individualism is a form of homesickness.*

As Unitarian Universalists we might add three additional idolatries that have afflicted our denomination with homesickness. These are "the idolatry of intellect and reason devoid of heart and soul," "the idolatry of works without faith," and "the idolatry of diversity."

The use of intellect and reason is not wrong. A mature faith needs to stand the test of intellect and reason. For individuals who are highly rational—and this includes many who are religious liberals—knowledge may be our primary spiritual path. As a spiritual path, knowledge centers upon wisdom. True wisdom is characterized by humility in knowledge rather than pride in knowledge. The Unitarian Universalist idolatry of intellect and reason is one of pride in knowledge. This pride sometimes manifests itself as intellectual elitism and intellectual self-righteousness.

The idolatry of intellect and reason stands as a real stumbling block for many religious liberals homesick for relevant spirituality. By a stumbling block, I mean that the misuse of intellect and reason can make it difficult to see the spiritual in life; the misuse of intellect and reason can make it difficult to embrace the mystical in creation; the misuse of intellect and reason can make it difficult to witness the Holy in and around us. Intellect and reason must be interwoven with heart and soul for true wisdom and spirituality to find expression. *The idolatry of intellect and reason devoid of heart and soul is a form of Unitarian Universalist homesickness.*

Attend most any General Assembly plenary session or read the resolutions that get passed from these sessions and one can witness the idolatry of works without faith in action. It appears that many modern Unitarian Universalists genuinely believe that love, community, and responsibility can be created by legislation. Social action is not synonymous with faith. Effective social action is only effective when it is a byproduct of faith. *The idolatry of works without faith is a form of Unitarian Universalist homesickness.*

Strength in diversity is not an exponential truth. Modern Unitarian Universalism has taken the notion of diversity to an extreme. Modern Unitarian Universalist diversity has become a weakness rather than strength. My friend and colleague John Morgan expresses this best of all in his article "Advice to Friends about Diversity," which appeared in the August 1992 issue of the *Universalist Herald*. John writes:

> Does anything go? Are there any limits to who can become a member of your meeting? These are the questions that constitute membership in a religious community, and are as old as religious communities. Open doors can sometimes be revolving doors when becoming part of a religious community is the same as joining the Kiwanis Club. And, to be honest, some Kiwanis Clubs are more spiritual than some congregations I've seen. There is a dangerous tendency among persons who express values of toleration to refrain from offending others by questioning their religious views; we can become passive observers of the latest fads or quick fixes in the name of toleration.

John goes on to write:

> Open doors will become revolving doors if people do not feel grounded within the sacred ground of their own tradition. The door to the future of our movement is one in which we learn to live in the tension between being open to new friends yet express-

ing a spiritual tradition that has served us for many centuries. We need to be much clearer about who we are, what we will and what we won't tolerate, and whether or not we are here to conform to the world or transform it.

Have we not as Unitarian Universalists made an idolatry of diversity? *The idolatry of diversity is a form of Unitarian Universalist homesickness.*

My thesis in this evening's sermon is that our yearning for that which we call home is much more than mere sentimentality or nostalgia. Our yearning for that which we call home comes from the very core of our being. Our yearning for that which we call home is in its very essence a spiritual calling. And in traditional theological language, our yearning for that which we call home is a yearning for the Holy, for that which some of us call God.

I believe that the Universalist faith offers hope and a remedy for homesick religious liberals as well as hope and a remedy for a homesick nation. I believe that many of the folks who have participated, traveled long distances, and donated personal funds in attending and supporting our Universalist Convocation effort have done so out of a sense of homesickness within the Unitarian Universalist Association. I suspect that many of you seated in this chapel this evening believe, or at least hope, that within the Universalist faith there is a remedy for this denominational homesickness. There are four aspects of Universalism that I wish to share with you this evening that I believe offer this hope and remedy.

1. The first aspect of Universalism that offers hope and a remedy is the affirmation of the Holy. Whether we term this sacred dimension of reality God, Divine Law, or Mystery of the Universe, Universalism, nonetheless, affirms the holiness in life and living. In affirming the holy, the Universalist faith is comfortable with the religious language of other denominations grounded in the Judeo-Christian tradition. Religious language such as God, sin, prayer, spirituality, guilt, and forgiveness has meaning within the Universalist tradition. But we are not limited to the Judeo-Christian tradition. Universalism transcends the Judeo-Christian tradition. Universalism sees spirituality as universal. We can find beauty and meaning in the spiritual language of any of the world's religious traditions. The Universalist affirmation of the Holy is our link to the faith traditions of our brothers and sisters worshipping in the Christian churches across the street as well as our brothers and sisters worshipping in the cathedrals, the mosques, the synagogues, and the shrines all across this planet.

2. The second aspect of Universalism that offers hope and a remedy is the affirmation of the power of love. Universalism can help foster a mature and genuine understanding of love. The Universalist faith stresses values and goals that foster mature love. Universalism encourages people to trust each other, to accept other people, and to accept ourselves. Universalism teaches that mature love is based on cooperation and respect for the integrity of the other person and not on manipulation and exploitation. The mature love which this faith nourishes is based on a willingness to take risks with people, to reach out and touch the mystery of another human being. In a society that has become homesick from worshipping the idea of independence, the mature love fostered by the Universalist faith stresses interdependence and community. In cities and towns across this nation where neighbors live in fear of and in isolation from one another, the Universalist values of interdependence and community offer hope and a remedy.

3. The third aspect of Universalism that offers hope and a remedy is the affirmation of the sacrificial spirit. This affirmation of the sacrificial is aptly expressed in the Washington Declaration of 1935 when we affirm the power of persons of good will and sacrificial spirit to overcome all evil and progressively establish the kingdom of God. Economists agree that the next decade will be a time of sacrifice for all Americans. At issue is in how just and fair of a manner will this sacrifice be administered, and more importantly, will this sacrifice reflect a sacrificial spirit on the part of our people? Or will this sacrifice be undertaken with bitterness, reluctance, anger, and hate among the American people? Learning to embrace a sacrificial spirit will offer hope and a remedy for all Americans as we approach the twenty-first century.

4. The fourth aspect of Universalism that offers hope and a remedy is the affirmation of the divinity in all people. When asked whether or not a Universalist believes that Jesus was the Son of God, many Universalists have responded "yes" only to add "but we believe that all people are children of God." It is the Universalist affirmation of the divinity in all people that is the basis of the Universalist belief in the supreme worth of every human personality. The Universalist faith stresses that there is the possibility for goodness in all people. There is an aspect of the Holy in each and every one of us. Our challenge is in recognizing the Holy, claiming the Holy, and allowing the Holy expression in our life and in our living. And in expressing the Holy, we cannot help but express love. Universalism teaches the doctrine of love and the positive power of love in human relationships. One cannot love in isolation. To love we must be in relationship with others. To love we must be in community. To love, and to know love, is to experience home.

"Blessed are the homesick," wrote the theologian Helmut Thielicke, "for they shall come home."

Perhaps there is some goodness in our individual homesickness, our cultural homesickness, and our denominational homesickness. The very force of homesickness is that in it the feeling of loss is recognized. Once we can identify homesickness for what it is, we know not only what we hold most dear, but also the need to try and get back to it and restore what is good and needed in life.

For the Prodigal Son, his homesickness "brought him to himself" and was the means of his salvation, and his story thereby is the story of all humanity. "Home" is our moral base. "Home" is where we belong. Homesickness that is recognized for what it is can stand as a lighthouse to beam us back home.

But I think that it is important that we differentiate between home and nostalgia for home. There is nothing wrong with nostalgia. I am a nostalgic person. You can easily see this if you ever walk into my office at the Outlaw's Bridge parsonage (that is if you can find a path through the boxes and books that often cover the floor of the parsonage office). I have a glassed bookshelf against one wall of the office loaded with nothing more than mementos. Upon the shelves are Boy Scout and Cub Scout badges, coffee mugs, matchbooks and packages of sugar from around the world, newspaper clippings, photographs, army medals and badges, two empty Korean beer cans, three never-opened Billy Beer cans, and an assortment of other mementos that only have meaning to me. I have a bulletin board that holds everything except bulletins: old airline tickets, name labels from General Assemblies and other Unitarian Universalist events of years gone by, political campaign buttons from 1976 through 1992, alongside Christmas and birthday cards that are over a decade old. On a nearby shelf can be found numerous scrapbooks filled with photos and memories of people and events of years that have passed. I often entertain myself by sitting in my office and looking over these collections. Each item brings back a memory. It is nostalgic and it is enjoyable.

But regardless of how pleasant the memory, regardless of how clear and crisp the photo, I know that these mementos recall a past that is no more. I can never and will never return to that place in time from which my memento rekindles a memory.

Nostalgia for the way Universalism used to be offers neither hope nor a remedy for the homesickness that pervades our nation and our denomination. It is important that we realize this fact.

Early Universalists often called their faith the religion of Jesus rather than the religion about Jesus. In 1992, we need to discern whether the faith we call Universalism is in fact the Universalist faith or is it a religion about the Universalist faith? Is this Universalist Convocation effort an attempt to promote and spread the good news of Universalism or are we more interested in preserving our heritage as a memento from the past? Is it churches we wish to build or is it museums?

One of the better films that I have watched in the past several years was the Academy Award winner *The Trip to Bountiful*. It is a beautiful story of an elderly woman whose last wish is to return to her childhood home before she dies. We find her living in a large urban city apartment with her son and daughter-in-law. It is not a pleasant situation. The discontented and nagging daughter-in-law treats the older woman like a child. The son is disillusioned with both his marriage and life in general and does little to intervene with his mother's treatment. Bountiful, Texas, was the older woman's childhood home, and in her memory she imagines Bountiful is as it was when she left it years earlier. She plans and schemes, waiting for her chance to return to the place and the life she knew, wanting only to embrace the memories of her past. Eventually, she does make her escape, and the adventure is in following her in a desperate attempt to get home. She first tries to go by train but finds that there are no longer any passenger trains that travel anywhere near Bountiful. Next she attempts to purchase a bus ticket, and she can't believe the person behind the ticket counter when she is told there is no longer bus service to Bountiful.

"This can't be!" she exclaims.

She does manage to purchase a bus ticket to a town several miles from Bountiful. She decides she will telephone an old friend in Bountiful to meet her at the bus station in this nearby town. All night she travels by bus on her way back home. In the wee morning hours she arrives in the nearby town. As she tries to telephone this old Bountiful friend from years gone by, she learns that this friend had been buried the previous day. We also learn that this dead friend had been the last living resident of Bountiful, Texas. The dear old lady does make it to Bountiful the next morning, but nothing is as she thought it would be. Bountiful, Texas, no longer existed except as a nostalgic memory.

The concern of some within the Unitarian Universalist Association is that the Universalist Convocation effort is a futile attempt to make a trip to Bountiful with Universalism. I hope this is not so. Universalism, since its beginning, has been a faith for the future. Think of old Thomas Potter. There was nothing nostalgic about his building a meeting house near Barnegat Bay. He was looking to the future, not to the past.

Nostalgia for Universalism offers neither hope nor a remedy for our homesickness. What is needed is the Universalist faith—the same faith that captured the hearts and minds of folks like Thomas Potter, John Murray, Hosea Ballou, George de Benneville, and many of your parents, grandparents, and great grandparents of years ago. It is right and proper that we enjoy a nostalgic appreciation for our past, but we must differentiate between nostalgia and faith. They are not the same. We cannot move forward so long as we insist on living in our previous history.

I want to express this evening my conviction that within that which we call Universalism may be found a remedy both for cultural and denominational homesickness. I chose the scripture selections from 2 Corinthians 4 because I see parallels between the Universalist faith and the faith that Paul is attempting to describe. Paul writes:

> We are like clay jars in which this treasure is stored. The real power comes from God and not from us. We often suffer, but we are never crushed. Even when we don't know what to do, we never give up. (2 Cor 4:7–8)

And verses 13 and 16 could speak for any one of us as we proclaim the Universalist faith: "I spoke because I had faith. We have that same kind of faith . . . we never give up."

The news wires carried the following story a few years ago:

> The large painting of icebergs hung on the wall of a boys' home in Manchester, England, almost unnoticed for years. Needing money for some improvements at the home, the institution's director decided to sell the painting to raise a few pounds and sent a color photograph of the painting to Sotheby Parke Bernet in London.
>
> The art world was stunned. The 64-inch by 112-inch painting "Icebergs" or "The Frozen North" by the famous American landscape artist Fredrick Church had been missing for over a century and had been long sought by art connoisseurs. And the boys' home

stands to make more than just a few pounds from the painting. In fact, it is expected to break the current record price of $980,000 for an American painting when it is auctioned in New York.

The painting qualified as a piece of valuable art since the day it was painted. The fact it hung unnoticed and largely unappreciated for years didn't depreciate it, for the painting was still *intrinsically* qualified as art.

So it is with the Universalist faith. Universalism qualifies as the religious faith that America yearns for today. But does not the word *Universalist* merely hang within the label Unitarian Universalist Association as did Fredrick Church's painting hang on the wall of a boys' home in Manchester, England?

The Universalist faith continues to have a gospel (which is another word for "good news"), and there are many Americans and Unitarian Universalists needing to hear the good news of Universalism. Universalism offers the spiritual depth and the sense of the Holy that many contemporary religious liberals find lacking in modern Unitarian Universalism. Universalism can, indeed, be a remedy for homesick religious liberals.

No man or woman is an island. You can't go it alone. Our existence has a social character about it. Friendly interchange grounded in love constitutes the spiritual life of friends, family, and other communities. Where there is love, there is God. Where there is love, there is home. We feed each other's faith and we give to one another the sense of home.

What does it take to be a home? To be a home, our churches, congregations, and fellowships must be places where both eager and weary searchers, skeptic souls, inquisitive thinkers, and great minds sometimes spiritually blinded by their own intellect, can all find direction, nurture, and support in discovering that which many of us call God.

Our churches, congregations and fellowships need to be places where the Holy is revered; where love is both taught and practiced; where sacrificial spirit is prevalent; and where each and every individual is recognized for his or her goodness and worth.

Where there is love, there is God. Where there is love, there is home. May we discern Universalist nostalgia from Universalist faith. May we take to our congregations the Universalist faith. May we look to our future and not dwell on our past. Let us proclaim the good news of Universalism. It is a homesickness remedy that our fellow Unitarian Universalists desperately need. May 1993 be the year in which Unitarian Universalism is reintroduced to the Universalist faith.

Delivered on October 16, 1992, Universalist Convocation 1992, Chapel, Shelter Neck, North Carolina.

5

In Praise of Doubt

Genesis 19:1–26

IN GENESIS 19 IS found the story of Lot, Lot's wife, and the destruction of Sodom and Gomorrah. It's a familiar biblical story. Sodom and Gomorrah were wicked cities, and Lot and his family were found to be the only righteous people in the entire two cities.

There are actually only twenty-six verses that deal with the story of Lot, and obviously there must have been more conversation between Lot, Lot's wife, and the two angels than what is recorded in these twenty-six verses.

Well, I'd like for us to briefly go back to that day, long ago, when Lot met the two angels on one of the streets of Sodom. (You know, we religious liberals often pride ourselves on the long list of distinguished individuals who have been associated with either Unitarianism or Universalism. However, one name that is never mentioned, but perhaps should be included, is that of Lot's wife. For in many ways, Lot's wife may represent the first biblical forerunner to liberal religion.)

Well, back to Sodom. Here we have Lot sitting on the sidewalk of one of the streets. Try and imagine a 1970s version of New York City Times Square or a Fayetteville, North Carolina's Hay Street existing in Old Testament days: Triple X rated shows, open prostitution, drug sales, maybe even some gambling on the sidewalks—perhaps you can imagine a picture of what Sodom was like. And here's Lot, sitting on the side of the street, and up walk two men—strangers in town—and in the course of the conversation they convince Lot that (1) they are angels, (2) that

God is going to destroy the city, and (3) that Lot and his family must leave immediately.

Well, Lot returns home that evening.

"Wife, I'm home."

"Lot, supper has been ready for the past hour. Why are you late?"

"I've been talking to two angels on the street."

"Oh, what sex were these angels?"

"Well, I guess they were male angels. They looked like men. Their clothes were different from the clothes of other men in town. At first I thought they were strangers—until they told me that they were angels sent by God."

"Lot, why would God send two angels to talk to you?"

"Wife, God is not pleased with this wicked city. And furthermore, he has found that we are the last remaining righteous family living in Sodom. He sent the two angels to warn us that he is going to destroy Sodom and that we must move."

"But Lot, we almost have this house paid for. The children like it here."

"Wife, we are going to move!"

"When are we to leave?"

"We must leave tonight!"

"Leave tonight? Lot, you could never sell this house that quickly. We couldn't even pack our furniture up by tonight."

"We're not going to sell the house. Also, we're leaving the furniture. The two angels said that we are to only take what we can carry on our backs."

"Sure, we take what we can carry on our backs and leave our nice house, our furniture, most of our food, our home, to two men who claim to be angels that you just happened to meet on the street this evening. Lot, don't you see? Those two so-called angels are con men."

"Wife, you have said enough! We leave and we leave tonight!"

So Lot and his wife and family pack what they can carry on their backs and begin to depart the city. The two angels are to remain at their home. But as they leave, the angels warn Lot and his family not to look back, but to hurry as quickly as possible to the distant hills.

Lot's wife perhaps thought, "Sure, you don't want us to look back—look back and see you two moving into our house!"

And Lot's wife doubted. She had to look back. And what happens when Lot's wife looks back is a tragic story. For in her questioning spirit and honest doubt, perhaps the world's first religious liberal was turned into a pillar of salt!

Many times the story of Lot's wife is used by more fundamentalist Christians as a means of warning folks of the dangers of doubting church dogma and doctrine. From the New Testament comes the story of the doubting Thomas. Chapter 20 of the Gospel of John tells the story of Thomas, the one disciple who doubted the resurrection. From this story in the Gospel of John has evolved the term "doubting Thomas," and in many Christian churches the label "doubting Thomas" is not positive but rather has a negative connotation.

Like many of you—particularly those of you who were reared in churches other than the Universalist Church—I was labeled a "doubting Thomas" during my teenage years as a United Methodist. And it was my doubting of many of the beliefs and theology other Christians took as basic tenets of faith that eventually led me to becoming a Universalist. Some of you also found your way to Universalism through your "doubting" of other more orthodox faiths.

The topic of this morning's sermon is "In Praise of Doubt," and it is to the doubting Thomases of today and in this congregation as well as the doubting Thomases of history—beginning with Lot's wife—that this morning's sermon is dedicated.

In the words of Kenneth Patton, "to doubt is a valorous and necessary faith, for to doubt is to believe in the intelligence and inventive imagination of humanity." And in a different passage, Patton writes, "doubt moves us from where we are to what our children will become; doubt is a hoe loosening the soil about the stalk of growth."

Think about it! It is often from creative doubters that new ideas, new inventions, and new solutions to problems evolve.

It was Columbus in 1492 who doubted the common belief that the Earth was flat and that if one sailed too far from land there would be a point at which the ship and crew would fall off the side of the Earth. Columbus' doubt resulted in the discovery of North America.

It was the astronomer Copernicus who in the early 1500s doubted the commonly held belief of his time that the earth was the center of the universe, and from this doubt, Copernicus developed the theory that Earth and the other planets revolved around the sun.

It was Michael Servetus, Spanish theologian of the 1500s, who doubted the Christian doctrine of the Trinity. And though he was burned at the stake in Geneva, Switzerland, for his doubt on charges of heresy, his thought and writings had a great influence toward the formal organization of European Unitarianism.

It was John Murray in the late 1700s who doubted the theological doctrine of divine election and eternal hell. He preached of universal salvation and his preaching led to the formation of the Universalist Church of America.

On a cold December day in 1955 in Montgomery, Alabama, a black woman named Rosa Parks doubted that she should have to give up her bus seat to a white passenger. Her doubt led to the repeal of many such discrimination laws in the Southern states of America.

And then it was the eloquent back Baptist minister Martin Luther King Jr. who until his assassination in Memphis, Tennessee, in the spring of 1968, devoted his life to his doubt that black and poor people should be treated as second-class citizens in the United States of America.

The list could go on and on of the names of famous doubters and the new ideas, new inventions, and new solutions to problems that evolved from their doubts.

The commonly held notion of many Christians is that doubting is symptomatic of a lack of faith. Cynicism may be symptomatic of a lack of faith, but honest doubt can be a healthy component of faith.

Tilden Edwards writes about the doubting-faith path in his book *Spiritual Friend*. He calls doubting the "fighting it all the way" faith path. This is the spiritual path of the skeptic or doubter. He writes that the skeptic's great strength is in smashing idols and challenging all hypocrisies. By clearing the path of false gods, the skeptic or doubter can eventually, without conscious intention, discover true divinity. But Edwards warns that at its worst, the skeptic path turns cynical and bitter or fearful and becomes no path at all.

How does the healthy doubter avoid becoming a cynic? By including some spiritual discipline in your life—that is, daily devotions, daily meditation or prayer—and being intellectually open to the possibility that all is not false. You must remain open to the belief that there is spiritual truth beyond the idols and hypocrisies.

It was Tennyson who wrote: "There lives more faith in honest doubt, believe me, than in half the creeds."

It is not easy to live with uncertainties.

It is not easy to live with doubt.

But life is uncertain and theologies are merely attempts to speculate on the meaning of life and death, the order of the universe, and the mystery of that which we call God.

Yes, I say let us praise doubt.

For there is the doubt of utterly sincere and honest minds who will not say what they do not think, and who in their intellectual integrity will not pretend to build belief until they have for it a foundation of certain fact.

Lot's wife, we do not know why you were turned into a pillar of salt. But we do not believe that this act was a result of that which we Universalists have come to call God. We respect and affirm your doubting spirit. And if we had been there with you, I am sure many of us would have also looked back.

6

Rediscovering the Meaning of Spirituality

As a deer gets thirsty for streams of water, I truly am thirsty for you, my God. In my heart, I am thirsty for you, the living God. (Psalms 42:1–2)

WHAT IS SPIRITUALITY? WILLIAM Least Heat Moon, the author of the recently popular book *Blue Highways*, tells the story of visiting a Trappist monastery where he talked with several of the monks. When questioned about spirituality, one of the monks told Moon that talking about the spiritual life was a waste of time. The monk said, "You just live it." This monk's life was a mixture of work, reflection, community, and worship. This was how he and the other monks found balance in their lives and came to experience that which they call God.

I begin with this illustration to try and set a tone for this sermon. Perhaps a sermon on spirituality and the spiritual life cannot be preached. But, nonetheless, it is my hope that the next twenty minutes of my sermon will at least sow some seeds that will later sprout in your own work, reflection, community, worship—and will later blossom into a definition of spirituality that is meaningful for you.

I also wish to clarify my own interest in the area of spirituality. I do not pretend to be an expert in this area. Nor do I pretend to be an example of the spiritual life. Four years ago I returned to seminary on a part-time basis primarily from a personal need for reexposure to theology and a need to re-look at my calling to the ministry. I was twenty-three years old when I completed my theological studies in 1976. And as I have grown in the ministry, and made a number of mistakes in the ministry, and seriously questioned the ministry as my life work—well, I have come to realize that due to my rather young age in seminary that I had been oblivious to many of the issues of theology and ministry that have surfaced for me since those seminary days. Personally I don't believe that I started thinking "theologically" about life until around the age of thirty—maybe I still haven't started thinking theologically! Nonetheless, it was around the age of thirty that the issues from which theology is woven came to have a new and deeper appreciation in my thought.

My return to the seminary classroom to pursue doctoral studies has been a real joy for me. For two years I attended an eight-hour day of classes every other week at Erskine Theological Seminary in Due West, South Carolina. During this time I was employed as an army chaplain at Fort Jackson, and I came to experience this day in the classroom as a real retreat. I enjoyed the vast majority of my classes, and I valued the collegiality and friendship that I found among my classmates—many of whom had also been out of seminary for ten or more years and who had had ten or more years of parish or chaplaincy experience, and most of whom, to my surprise, were also dealing with some of the same issues in ministry as I was.

It was in one of my first courses that I was introduced to the work of Urban Holmes, former Dean of the School of Theology of the University of the South. Prior to his death in 1981, Holmes was widely recognized as an authority in spiritual theology. It was in reading Holmes that I became excited about the areas of spirituality, spiritual directing, and spiritual theology. This interest led to other courses and has eventually led to my choosing spirituality as my area of focus for my dissertation. And although I have read numerous authors who have written on the subject of spirituality, I must admit that I continue to struggle to define for myself an adequate definition for the meaning of spirituality.

What is spirituality? It seems to me that many religious liberals experience some awkwardness and uncertainty in the use of terms such as *spiritual* and *spirituality*. Some religious liberals erroneously associate Christian spirituality with fundamentalism and dogmatism. Others may negate the relevance of spirituality and spiritual formation in the practice of a rational and modern faith.

Interestingly, fundamentalists also have problems with the term *spirituality*. For religious fundamentalists, the term *spirituality* stirs up associations with pantheism, meditation, and what is sometimes called the New Age movement. Christian spirituality is not New Age, but many New Age followers would be surprised to learn that some of what New Agers call New Age actually has roots in the Christian mystical tradition.

There is a hearing aid company that asks in its commercial: "Are you hearing sounds but not words?" When we approach the touchy and fuzzy area of spirituality, our first problem is the communications barrier. I can give you endless "sounds" about spirituality, but if they don't carry the meanings intended, they remain meaningless words, or worse, misinterpreted ones.

We cannot overcome this problem completely, since we are dealing with an area primarily of apprehension rather than of comprehension. There is the short parable in Anthony de Mello's book *The Song of the Bird* that illustrates this problem of apprehension. The title of this parable is "The Little Fish," and many of you have heard me read this parable before. It goes like this:

> "Excuse me," said one ocean fish to another, "You are older and more experienced than I, and will probably be able to help me. Tell me, where can I find this thing they call the Ocean? I've been searching for it everywhere to no avail."
>
> "The Ocean," said the older fish, "is what you are swimming in now."
>
> "Oh this? But this is only water. What I'm searching for is the Ocean," said the young fish, feeling quite disappointed as he swam away to search elsewhere.

The apprehension involved with the meaning of spirituality might resemble the little fish perceiving the ocean.

In his book *Spiritual Friend*, Tilden Edwards defines spirituality as "the most subtle dimension of our awareness and consciousness, where we sense ourselves belonging beyond our ego to a larger horizon of reality that impinges on all we are and do."

In his essay "What Does Spiritual Growth Mean, If Anything?" the Unitarian Universalist minister Bruce Southworth states that "most definitions of spirituality have something to do with living between polarities and extremes." Definitions of spirituality include awareness, balance, reconciliation, and wholeness.

This past Friday evening I had the opportunity to attend a lecture given by Matthew Fox. It was held at Trinity Episcopal Cathedral in downtown Columbia, South Carolina. Matthew Fox is a Dominican priest and is known by many for his writings about creation-centered spirituality. His views, although declared deviant by the Vatican, are helpful. I find creation-centered spiritual theology as very compatible with historical

Universalism. In defining spirituality, Matthew Fox speaks about balance, a balance that includes (1) a joyful embrace of the world and its beauty, (2) acceptance of pain and suffering, (3) creative activity wherein we are agents of divine living, and (4) compassionate action with efforts to make a more just world.

So much of life—especially in modern American culture—is not so much balance as it is a balancing act. Family, work, home, upkeep of home, budget! How does one remain whole in the midst of the distractions of life?

Pursuing those skills, habits, and attitudes that lead to a heightened awareness and a sense of balance and emanates in more compassionate living is what true spiritual growth and intentional spirituality mean.

Sometimes there is a tendency for both religious conservatives and religious liberals to associate "spirituality" exclusively with contemplative and/or monastic lifestyles.

During the past two years I've had the opportunity to participate in a couple of three-day retreats at an Episcopal monastery near Pineville, South Carolina. Along with joining the monks for their daily prayers and meditation, I and the other retreat guests shared with the monks the work of preparing three communal meals; assisted in the grinding of wheat for flour; helped in the blending of incense that the monastery sells for income; and assisted with other maintenance chores. All of us observed twelve hours of silence from early evening until the next morning.

From these contemplative retreat experiences, I will say, *yes*: intentional spirituality and spiritual growth can certainly be fostered in contemplative and monastic lifestyles, but it is not confined to either.

Spirituality and spiritual-growth experiences can be found in the ordinary, and sometimes the best places for developing one's spirituality may be those places where religion is least emphasized, such as these:

- Baking bread
- Tending a garden
- Doing woodwork
- Working with needle and thread
- Building a house
- Playing with a pet dog
- Feeding the hungry
- Visiting the sick
- Making music

These are but a few of the daily activities that can assume spiritual dimensions when each event is performed with intentional awareness.

In his book *If It Die*, André Gide describes the time when during a classroom lecture he observed a moth being reborn from its cocoon. Young André was filled with wonder, awe, and joy at this metamorphosis. With much enthusiasm he showed it to his professor who replied with a note of disapproval, "What! Didn't you know that a cocoon is the envelope of a butterfly? Every butterfly you see has come out of a cocoon. It's perfectly natural." Somewhat disillusioned, Gide wrote, "Yes, indeed, I know my natural history as well, perhaps better than he. . . . But because it was natural, could he not see that it was marvelous?"

Young Gide's awareness of the moth's rebirth might be considered a lesson in spirituality. Matthew Fox mentioned in his Friday lecture that in true spirituality—be it Christian or some other faith tradition—the joy of that spirituality must include awe and wonder.

Nature has much to teach about spirituality. The first step in experiencing the spirituality of nature is reverent observation. Even a leaf can speak of order and variety, complexity and symmetry. In the changing seasons and in every living plant and creature, there are opportunities for that awareness where we sense ourselves belonging beyond our ego to a larger horizon of reality—opportunities when we as little fish catch glimpses of the ocean and not just water.

I hope that what I mean by spirituality and spiritual growth is becoming a bit clearer. I admit that intentional spirituality is a curious thing. The world in which we live is often overwhelmed with a focus on the mundane with little regard for that which deepens life. The Quaker author Richard Foster in his book *Celebration of Discipline* writes that "superficiality is the curse of our age and that the doctrine of instant satisfaction is a primary spiritual problem."

Spirituality for many modern Americans has become something archaic, quaint, and antiquated. Spirituality for some is irrelevant at best or at worst a childish remnant of orthodox Christianity which does not liberate, but rather enslaves the human spirit.

There is also the image that being "spiritual" takes us out of the world or that being "spiritual" removes us from engagement with the world and its ills.

True spirituality is neither archaic, quaint, nor antiquated. True spirituality is not a mere remnant of orthodox Christianity. And true spirituality does not excuse us from the world and the problems of this world.

Within the Unitarian and Universalist traditions we could point to the Transcendentalists. The Transcendentalist movement of the 1800s could easily be identified by their commitment to an intentional spirituality, and yet many of the Transcendentalists were also known for their social activism. For example, Theodore Parker was very involved with the anti-slavery effort, and Margaret Fuller was a women's rights activist.

Also, it is a false spirituality when in using the term *spirituality* we take a Pollyanna view of life. A true spirituality involves balance. True spirituality involves balancing suffering with joy, ugliness with beauty, tragedy with blessings, evil with good, and death with life. A true spirituality seeks balance with the horror of the death and destruction caused by the cyclone that struck Bangladesh last week and the horror of death and destruction of war alongside those aspects of nature in which we experience beauty and creativity.

We find the emergence in our time of psychological vocabulary that speaks words such as awareness, perception, identity, integration, wholeness, and consciousness. All of these terms are a modern-day spiritual vocabulary because they speak of the human hunger to achieve balance and meaning.

Spiritual growth—connectedness in life's mystery—occurs in multiple ways, and there are many contemporary ways of talking about it. But as the Trappist monk in my opening quote from *Blue Highways* reminds us, talking is easy; the thing is getting on with life and with living.

The question that may remain for many of you is, how do we pursue an intentional spirituality?

Unfortunately, there is no one answer to this question. There is no one path for spiritual growth. There are multiple paths. Let me introduce to you four different paths discussed by Tilden Edwards in *Spiritual Friend*. Perhaps this may help you understand your own approach and perhaps create an interest in you to explore further a particular path.

1. First, there is the path of devotion. By this I mean there are among us those who have a clear, personal, and intimate sense of that which is called God. Prayer, praise, thanksgiving, devotion, and aesthetic sensitivity are hallmarks of this path. Creative artists, painters, poets, musicians and others may follow this path without particular reference to God. Either way, the path of devotion is one means to pursue spiritual growth, and it may include a variety of devotional and worship practices including prayer, meditation, readings, or in a more secular fashion the arts. For others, the pursuit of God in beauty will include nature mysticism.

2. A second spiritual path is that of action. Moral and ethical concerns may dominate. On the action path we especially give ourselves over to our neighbor (both our human neighbors and our neighbors in nature). At its best, this path channels our spiritual yearning into self-forgetful, risk-taking, community-building human concern and action. Martin Luther supposedly once said that he had so much to do one day that he would have to spend at least three hours in prayer in order to have energy to get everything done. What Luther was alluding to was that for social action to be an effective spiritual path it must be balanced to some degree with aspects of the devotional path.

3. Third is the path of knowledge. To grow spiritually, some of us who are highly rational look to theology and philosophy to help us understand the world and our place in it. Knowledge can give us balance and perspective and heartfelt connection. The path of knowledge centers on wisdom.

The spiritual path of knowledge forks into two approaches: The first is centered on analytical knowledge. Theology, philosophy, and the sciences discipline such thinking.

The second fork moves toward intuitive knowledge, a subtle awareness of the truth that seems to be there without the involvement of our intellect. Contemplation, Zen Buddhism, the arts, parables, and psychic powers express or aim for this path.

I will add, however, that the path of knowledge is not one of pride in knowledge but is rather one of humility in knowledge. The pride that some find in knowledge is not a spiritual path at all, but it is rather another form of materialism or consumerism. For example, is a student's primary goal in college or university the attainment of a specific degree or is the primary goal the gaining of knowledge? Attending school for the sake of attaining a degree or academic title might be considered materialism, whereas studying for the sake of gaining greater wisdom might be the spiritual path of knowledge.

4. Finally there is the path that has been called "fighting it all the way." This is the path of the skeptic. The skeptic's great strength is in smashing idols and challenging all hypocrisies. By clearing the path of false gods, the skeptic can eventually, without conscious intention, discover true divinity. At its worst, the skeptic path turns cynical and bitter or fearful and becomes no path at all. The disguised energy of spiritual yearning reveals itself only as a vague emptiness channeled into sensual drive and work, or lapsing into laziness. The skeptic path can lead one to eventually experience that which we call God or it can become no path at all.

(1) Devotion, (2) social action, (3) knowledge, (4) skepticism—all four of these paths belong to the human potential in each of us. Probably we walk along each at some point in our lives. Usually only one path will be dominant in our lives at any one time—sometimes for a lifetime.

Our personalities will have much to say about this. If our personality is highly intuitive, then we are likely to gravitate toward the path of intuitive awareness; if we are strong thinkers, toward the path of reason or the path of the skeptic; if strong feelers (that is, we show emotions readily) then we may move toward either the path of devotion or the path of action.

I close with a *Peanuts* cartoon. Charlie Brown is at the doctor's psychiatric booth where Lucy offers help for five cents. The doctor is "IN" as Lucy sits at her table. Charlie Brown asks, "What can you do when life seems to be passing you by?"

Lucy answers, "Follow me. . . . I want to show you something." So he gets up and follows her. Standing upon a grassy hillside with fluffy clouds all about them, she says, "See the horizon over there? See how big this world is? See how much room there is for everybody?" Then she asks, "Have you seen any other worlds?"

Charlie Brown answers, "No."

Lucy asks, "As far as you know, this is the only world there is, right?" "Right."

"There are no other worlds for you to live in . . . Right?" she asks.

"Right," he says.

"You were born to live in this world . . . Right?"

"Right!"

"WELL, LIVE IN IT, THEN!!" she declares and pauses. "Five cents, please!"

And, when all is said and done, that is what spirituality and spiritual growth are about: not talking, but you finding your path and living it and living in the world.

Delivered at Homecoming Service 1991, Outlaw's Bridge Universalist Church, Seven Springs, North Carolina.

7

Faith, Hope, and Love, But the Second Greatest of These Is Hope!

God promised Abraham a lot of descendants. And when it all seemed hopeless, Abraham still had faith in God and became the ancestor of many nations. Abraham's faith never became weak, not even when he was nearly a hundred years old. He knew that he was almost dead and that his wife Sarah could not have children. But Abraham never doubted or questioned God's promise. His faith made him strong, and he gave all the credit to God. Abraham was certain that God could do what he had promised. (Rom 4:18–21)

But I will bless those who trust me. They will be like trees growing beside a stream—trees with roots that reach down to the water, and with leaves that are always green. They bear fruit every year and are never worried. (Jer 17:7–8)

For now there are faith, hope, and love. But of these three, the greatest is love. (1 Cor 13:13)

FAITH, HOPE, AND LOVE are what the Apostle Paul attributes as qualities of the spiritual life. Paul tells us that love is the greatest of these three qualities, and as Universalists we have proclaimed the message of love as central to our religion. But what can we say about the spiritual quality of hope? We find that hope is a theme throughout the Bible second only to love. What is the meaning of hope in our faith journey?

In *Macbeth*, Shakespeare writes:

Tomorrow, and tomorrow, and tomorrow
Creeps in the petty pace from day to day,
To the last syllable of recorded time;
And all our yesterdays have lighted fools

> The way to dusty death. Out, out, brief candle!
> Life's but a walking shadow, a poor player
> That struts and frets his hour upon the stage,
> And then is heard no more; it is a tale
> Told by an idiot, full of sound and fury,
> Signifying nothing. (*Macbeth* V.v.19–28)

This writing by Shakespeare is pretty hopeless stuff, isn't it? Spiritual hope is not to be thought of as an uncertain feeling of mingled longing and misgiving, as when we say that we hope it will be a fine day tomorrow, knowing that it may well be nothing of the kind. Spiritual hope is a glad confidence in good things to come. It is sure, not tentative.

Paul Tillich, one of the better thinkers and theologians of modern times, preached a sermon at Harvard's Memorial Church in March 1965 entitled "The Right to Hope." He introduced the sermon in these words:

> Hope is a permanent force in every man, a driving power as long as he lives. . . . We may wonder why it is so seldom that philosophers and theologians speak about hope. They don't ask what kind of force it is that creates and maintains hope, even if everything seems to contradict it. Instead, they devalue hope by calling it wishful thinking or utopian fantasy.
>
> But nobody can live without hope, even if it were only for the smallest things which give some satisfaction even under the worst of conditions, even in poverty, sickness, and social failure. Without hope, the tension of our life toward the future would vanish, and with it, life itself. We would end in despair, a word that originally meant "without hope," or in deadly indifference.

None of you as Universalists ever deal with hopelessness, do you? Of course you do. It was the Unitarian, Henry David Thoreau, who wrote in *Walden*, "The mass of men lead lives of quiet desperation."

Ben Curtis, who teaches personality and theology at Vanderbilt Divinity School, says that most of us go through life with low level feelings of despair and hopelessness for two reasons: we feel devalued and/or we feel misunderstood.

How many of you are fans of Woody Allen? Woody Allen is noted for his treatment of hopelessness in many of his films. In the movie *Annie Hall*, the main character, played by Woody Allen, says this about life: "We have two alternatives. One leads to hopelessness, alienation, and despair.

The other leads to total destruction. Let us hope we have the wisdom to make the right choice."

Hope—what is the importance of hope in one's life? Perhaps the need for hope is not limited to human beings. Scientists have done studies with rats in which they have found that rats drown in a jar of water in a little over three minutes, when after making several swims around the perimeter of the jar they evidently give up. However, other rats were placed in a glass container, with the identical depth of water and angle of slant in the glass as that of a jar, but that includes several glass passageways all of which merely lead to just another glass passageway. Rats placed in this maze of glass passageways will continue to swim for over thirty-six hours before they drown. Those rats swimming in the maze of passageways continue to apparently have hope for eventually reaching a place whereby they can escape from the water. As an animal rights activist, I do wish the scientists conducting this experiment could have found a means of testing their hypothesis short of having to allow all the rats to drown. However, this experiment does seem to indicate that even animal life is impacted by hope.

Dr. William M. Buchholz writing in *The Western Journal of Medicine* tells the story of eating breakfast one morning and overhearing two oncologists discussing the papers they were to present that day at the national meeting of the American Society of Clinical Oncology. Of course, oncology deals with the subject of cancer, and oncologists are medical doctors who specialize in cancer treatment. However, in listening to these two oncologists speak, Dr. Buchholz heard one complain bitterly:

"You know, Bob, I just don't understand it. We used the same drugs, the same dosage, the same schedule, and the same entry criteria. Yet I got a twenty-two percent response rate and you got a seventy-four percent. That's unheard of for lung cancer. How do you do it?"

The other doctor responded: "We're both using Etoposide, Platinal, Oncovin, and Hydroxyurea. You call yours EPOH. I reverse that. I tell my patients I'm giving them HOPE. Sure, I tell them this is experimental and we go over the long list of side effects together. But I emphasize that we have a chance. As dismal as the statistics are for non-small cell, there are always a few percent who do really well."

Hope. Hopefulness is an important aspect of one's faith journey. Hope is second only to love. But how do we get hope? How does one attain hopefulness?

In Judaism, there is a rabbinic teaching that says that we should carry two pieces of paper on us at all times. One piece of paper we should keep in our left pocket and the other in our right pocket, and we should remove each piece of paper and read what is written upon it every day. On the piece of paper in our left pocket should be written the words "I am only dust and ashes." We read this to keep us humble. On the piece of paper in our right pocket should be written the words "It was for me and me alone that the Lord created the universe." The second reading is to give us hope.

As Universalists we affirm that Jesus was Son of God as we all are children of God. We affirm to try and live the religion of Jesus and not the religion about Jesus. Yet I think we all forget the significance of this Universalist teaching. Every one of us has the potential to express the consciousness and spirituality that was expressed by Jesus. We all suffer from spiritual amnesia from time to time. We forget who we are. Spiritual amnesia robs us of hope.

William Blake wrote, "We are put on this earth but a short time to bear the beams of love."

Hope is at the heart of existence. It seeks an outlet at every level of human life. Ernst Bloch writes, "Where there is life, there is hope. And where there is hope, there is religion."

Remember the story of the beginnings of Universalism in this country. May we never forget the hopefulness of Thomas Potter. Potter hoped and believed that God would send him a minister who preached Universalism. And remember John Murray, a sad and hopeless minister who sailed to America to forget his past and to die. Yet it was with Thomas Potter persuading Murray, and perhaps the mystery of God working on John Murray, that Murray was led to regaining *hope*. And it was with this new hope that John Murray eventually founded the Universalist Church of America.

Hope—we can't live for long without it.

An eighteen-year-old Brooklyn College student protested to her elders, "If people are right in saying that these are the best years of my life, then I don't know that I care to stay around and see the rest!"

Some people feel that way about facing the future. If it's anything like the past, they don't care to stick around for it. Such people are literally hopeless! Consider, on the other hand, Helen Worth of Portville, New York, a grandmother, teacher, and an active United Methodist. At fifty-four, she discovered that she has AIDS because of a blood transfusion she had received seven years ago. Her faith has been challenged during the past two years since she received that news. Persons who are HIV positive such as Worth respond to such news with a variety of emotions: despair, depression, anger, bitterness, and in some, in time, acceptance and hope. The struggle with such diverse feelings is natural and impacted by the state of their health and support of friends and family, and their own faith struggle. Helen Worth wrote a statement that reflects on her own doubt and hope:

> I am over the initial shock now. Whole days pass when I am able to forget my adversity. Now I have an answer to the question I used to ask God, "Why me?"
>
> For God has opened many doors providing new challenges, commitments, and opportunities; A college level job teaching teachers to teach; Community speaking engagements; and sometimes I am even asked to preach. . . . But, I would be remiss without saying that sometimes I am sad, I am afraid of the future, and, at times, even mad! However, with the grace of God these moments do not last . . . for new opportunities await me. My uncertainties are assigned to the past. And instead of lamenting on the question, "Why me?" I ask, "Why not me, Lord?" "Yes, Lord, why not me?"

In reality, Universalism was founded as much upon hope as it was love. In the words of John Murray, "Give them, not hell, but hope and courage!" This was from a hopeful John Murray. This was the John Murray after his encounter with Thomas Potter. It was this hopeful Universalism that led to the formation of the Universalist Church of America.

The full quote goes like this: "You possess only a small light, but uncover it, let it shine, use it in order to bring more light and understanding to the hearts and minds of men and women. Give them, not hell, but hope and courage."

May we as Universalists reaffirm and rekindle the spiritual quality of hope in our faith journey.

8

Celebrating a Universalist Universal Easter

Tᴴɪꜱ ᴍᴏʀɴɪɴɢ I ʜᴏᴘᴇ to successfully propose a new way of looking at Easter. Traditionally, Easter has been an awkward holiday for
Universalists. For the majority of Christians, Easter is the day of days:
the day of the resurrection of Jesus. The Apostle Paul considered Easter a
fundamental fact of faith. In 1 Corinthians 15:17, Paul preaches, "If Christ
has not been raised, your faith is futile." For most Christians, Easter is
celebrated as the day the sting of death was conquered.

Most Universalists doubt the physical resurrection of Jesus from
the tomb. Whether or not Jesus was resurrected from the dead, our
Universalist theology negates any importance to this event in relation to
salvation and immortality. If there is a human soul (and I believe there is),
the fact of the matter as to whether or not this human soul exists in some
shape, fashion, or form after our physical bodies die is not determined by
whether or not Jesus emerged from his tomb the third day following his
crucifixion. Immortality either is or isn't—regardless of the events of that
first Easter.

Through the years, Universalists have tried to modify this resurrection theme. We have had services that allude to the natural theology of
resurrection found in the world of nature in the spring season. We have
conducted flower communion services. We have also had services that
reflect upon the life and teachings of Jesus of Nazareth, making Easter
something of a memorial service to Jesus.

However, it occurred to me these past couple of weeks as I thought
about this sermon that the true theme of Easter is universal. At the heart
of Easter theology lays the basis of all our religions and philosophies. And
as Universalists, we can find meaning in Easter, a meaning that transcends
the celebration of the return of spring, a meaning that transcends flower

communion services, and a meaning that transcends memorials to Jesus of Nazareth.

At the heart of Easter is the fact of human death. How we come to confront the fact of our own deaths, and how we are able to find meaning and hope despite the fact of our own deaths—these are the universal Easter issues. The human dilemma of finding hope and meaning despite the certainty of death is an Easter theme that transcends Holy Week and the spring season. This theme is the basis of all theology. It is a theme that challenges and mystifies each one of us from that time in early childhood when we first become aware of death until we later draw our last breaths.

It is a matter of debate whether animals have an awareness of mortality, but it is certain that humans alone among all living creatures know that they have to die. Yet human beings have an uncanny ability to ignore their own mortality. Sigmund Freud said, "We have difficulty visualizing the end of our existence. . . . deep down contemporary man does not really believe in his own death." The theologian Martin Heidegger observed that the proposition "all men and women are mortal" usually involves the implicit reservation "but not I."

The Unitarian Universalist minister Judith Walker-Riggs, writing in the March 1992 *First Days Record*, recalls an experience from the time when she was a member of the Unitarian Universalist Ministerial Fellowship Committee. All prospective Unitarian Universalist ministers must appear before this committee, and ministerial candidates must come prepared to respond to any number of questions concerning theology, ministry, academics, and personal life. She tells the story of one young man appearing before this committee who in response to a question about death began his reply, "Well, if I die . . ." and was met by a spontaneous joint shout of the entire committee, "If?"

The late Joseph Sitler was one of America's best known preachers and an eminent Lutheran theologian. Prior to his death, he wrote these well-crafted words:

> The fear of death, I'm convinced, is at the bottom of all apprehensions. To say of any of us that we do not fear death is a lie. To be human is to fear death. To love life is to hope and to wish not to leave it. And all people fear death. I think that is one of the most creative fears there is because it bestows a value, an affection and a gratitude for life which otherwise there would not be.

Dr. Sitler further writes that "this is what Psalm 90 means by the statement, 'So teach us to number our days that we may get a heart of wisdom.'"

Allow me the freedom to reexpress this verse from Psalm 90 to reflect this sermon's Easter theme: So teach us to number our days, in other words, may we become aware of our own deaths, that we may get a heart of wisdom, or in other words, that we may find hope and meaning in living. Thus we could rewrite this verse to read: "May we become aware of our own deaths, so that we may find hope and meaning in living."

Coming to terms with our own death gives meaning and maturity to our lives. In biological terms, death is a necessity. The awareness of the shortness of life on earth gives urgency to achievement and impetus to reach our goals before human powers diminish.

Carl Jung wrote, "Death is psychologically just as important as birth. As the arrow flies to the target, so life ends in death. . . . Shrinking away from it is something unhealthy and abnormal which robs the second half of life of its purpose."

The universal Easter theme involves confronting one's personal death and finding meaning and hope for living despite our physical mortality.

When psychologist Abraham Maslow had his first heart attack and realized his days were numbered, he wrote to a friend:

> My river never seemed so beautiful. The confrontation with death . . . and reprieve from it . . . makes everything look so precious, so sacred, so beautiful and I feel more strongly than ever the impulse to love it, to embrace it, and to let myself be overwhelmed by it. . . . Death, and its ever present possibility, makes love, passionate love, more possible. I wonder if we could love passionately, if ecstasy would be possible at all, if we knew we'd never die.

Life out of death, not life and death, but finding a will and zest for living despite death is the universal Easter theme.

How do *you* find hope and meaning in life despite the certain knowledge of later death? Your answer to that question defines the meaning of Easter for you. Think about it!

In his book, *The Death of Ivan Illych*, Leo Tolstoy describes the anguish of a man who discovers on his deathbed that he has wasted his life. Ivan Illych has always done the right things: he took the right job, married the right woman, had the proper number of children. But he has lived without passion, without conviction, without love. Dying, he realizes that he has never known real happiness. He has been so busy doing what was expected of him, that he never did the things that he truly wanted. He says: "What if my whole life had been wrong?" It occurs to him that the whole arrangement of his life, of his family, and all his social and official interest may have been false. He tries to defend all these things to himself and suddenly finds that there is nothing to defend, and he came down to a bitter end.

The awareness of Ivan Illych's own crucifixion came too late for Ivan Illych to discover his Easter.

I ask each one of you again: How do you find hope and meaning in life despite the certain knowledge of later death? Your answer to that question defines the meaning of Easter for you.

I like Paul Tsongas. He was my favorite among the 1992 Democratic presidential candidates. During his time as senator from Massachusetts he was recognized by both Democrats and Republicans as one of the best and brightest senators in our country. At the age of forty-two Senator Tsongas discovered that he had an incurable form of cancer. In one very moving passage from his book *Heading Home*, he describes something that happened to him at a family picnic. He wrote:

> I wanted to get away . . . so I jumped across some rock ledges to a large boulder too far out in the river for easy access. . . . it worked, and I lay on the large rock basking in the sun and allowed my mind to run free. Finally, I turned around and looked back to where my wife and the children were playing. That moment is seared in my mind, because it was the first time I envisioned them without me. On the rock, too far away to be part of them, I watched a scene which could easily have occurred with me gone. At first my reaction was sadness. How wonderful they all were and how much I yearned to be there always. If I was to be taken away from this scene permanently, the same activities would occur, except I would not be observing. . . . they might be repeating this day in the future without me. They all had their lives to live and too much to offer to be imprisoned by prolonged grief. . . . my initial shock at this realization gave way to comfort. I felt pleasure knowing that my presence would always be felt by my absence and that life would go on.

What Paul Tsongas is describing gives us a glimpse of his own Easter, and his is an Easter that is, in part, intertwined with family.

In the sermon "Rekindling the Faith," the Rev. Justin Lapoint states that

> One of the reasons the story of the death and resurrection of Jesus has such power is that it touches on the human need to know that beyond the present pain and ordeal is hope. The cry of Jesus from the Cross, "My God, My God, why have you forsaken me?" has been re-echoed in countless lives caught in pain and suffering.

Justin goes on to tell of the broken-hearted and world-weary John Murray arriving in the New World. Murray sailed to American having had a wife and baby child die before their time, and a brush with debtors' prison. Murray came to America with painful memories. Prior to meeting Thomas Potter, we see in Murray another Ivan Illych. Murray knew the crucifixion, but he had no Easter. Yet, through his meetings with Thomas Potter, Murray became a new person, reborn with hope and courage. The life of John Murray witnesses to the victory of the human spirit over tragedy and despair! Somehow in Potter's meeting house, Murray found his Easter.

I close with the question, How do you find hope and meaning in life despite the certain knowledge of later death? How do you find hope and meaning in life despite the certain knowledge of your own later crucifixion? Your answer to this question defines the meaning of Easter for you.

9

Finding Meaning in the Easter Cross

EASTER WEEKEND IS THE time when Christians all over the world commemorate the resurrection of Jesus on Easter Sunday. From the very beginning, Christians have proclaimed the bodily resurrection as a validation of all that Jesus taught and all that they believe. It is the foundation upon which all else in the Christian faith is based. For most Christians the cross is the preeminent symbol of the Easter weekend. For most Christians the cross symbolizes the theology of human salvation through the death of Jesus. For most Christians the cross reflects this same salvation theology whenever it is displayed or worn.

Easter can be an awkward time for Universalists. I personally feel better about celebrating Good Friday than I do Easter. I can relate to an observance that reflects upon the life, the teachings, and the death of Jesus of Nazareth. I have much admiration and respect for the lifestyle and teachings of Jesus. I find that the themes of most Christian Good Friday services are such that, as a Universalist, I am able to find meaning in what is said from the pulpit. The language and theology of our Universalist Communion service in which we will participate later this morning is actually more in keeping with Good Friday than it is Easter. Our Communion service is basically a memorial to Jesus of Nazareth. But Easter is another story—especially Easter sunrise services. It has been while attending and sometimes participating in Easter sunrise services that I have felt my greatest alienation from traditional Christianity. This morning we had an Easter sunrise service at the prison, and I was overjoyed that the other Protestant chaplain volunteered to lead this service.

Yet it is also at Easter sunrise services that I am reconfirmed as to my identity as a Unitarian Universalist. There is no church, other than a Universalist church, where I would rather be on Easter morning. Many of our neighbors celebrate the physical resurrection of Jesus this day. More than simply celebrating the resurrection of Jesus, most Christians see in the Easter weekend the basis of the Christian faith. They claim that it is in the death and resurrection of Jesus that God made a way for Christians, who accept Jesus Christ as their Savior, to be forgiven of their sins and have eternal life. For most Christians, Easter is the event that proves eternal life. Without the suffering and death of Jesus on the cross, followed by his resurrection, there would be no means by which we could be forgiven for our sins and have eternal life. Sometime around the age of thirteen, while still a member of the United Methodist Church, I realized that this Christian doctrine of atonement just didn't make any sense to me. It would be another ten years before I would discover Unitarianism and Universalism and learn that for both Unitarians and Universalists the doctrine of atonement didn't make much sense either. It's not that we do not believe in some form of immortality. The immortality of the human soul is a basic tenet of early Universalism. But for those of us who do lean toward some belief in immortality, our reason for doing so has little to do with the biblical account of the first Easter.

At Easter, many Universalists have modified this resurrection theme to reflect a natural theology of rebirth and resurrection as witnessed in the world of nature with the coming of spring. And as we look at other cultures and religions, we find that from time immemorial, the spring season has been the occasion of observances recognizing the victory of spring over winter and life over death. During this time of the year all plants, including cultivated ones, begin growth anew after the dormancy of winter. Animals are greatly affected too. They come out of their winter dormancy, or hibernation, and begin their nesting and reproducing activities.

Universalists can commemorate the life and teachings of Jesus of Nazareth in a Good Friday style communion service, and we can celebrate a modified resurrection theme on Easter Sunday. But the primary symbol of the Easter weekend is the cross. What about the symbol of the cross? Can we find meaning in the Easter cross?

For many of our neighbors, the cross has but one meaning. For most Protestant Christians the display of the cross signifies one's belief that salvation is possible only because of the death and resurrection of Jesus. However, the history of the cross as a religious symbol is much more complex. There are other meanings of this Easter symbol that can be quite compatible with Universalist thought.

The origin of the cross as a religious symbol is very old. Its actual beginnings as a symbol are unknown. We do know that before the Christian era, the cross was a mystical symbol for both the ancient Phoenicians and Egyptians.

According to Rosicrucian teachings, ancient Egyptian mystics created the symbol of the cross by standing upon a plain at sunrise, looking toward the East. There the Egyptian would raise his or her arms to a level with the shoulders in adoration of the Sun, the giver of life. Then, turning to face the west to salute the place where life ended, symbolically, he or she found that the arms and body, while in the act of salutation, formed a shadow on the ground, cast by the rising sun. The shadow was in the form of the cross, and to the Egyptian it meant that life was but a shadow. Later the Egyptians added a loop to the top of the cross. This formed what is now called the Egyptian cross, and it became a very important symbol of their rituals. It was their symbol of immortality or the continuity of life.

It is interesting that as a Protestant Christian symbol, the cross also symbolizes immortality. But for the Protestant Christian, this symbolism is tied to the crucifixion and the resurrection. One can't help but wonder if the modern interpretation of the cross as a symbol of eternal salvation, via Jesus as Savior, might not have its roots in the Egyptian mystical interpretation of the cross.

In ancient Judaism, the cross was a symbol of suffering in the form of persecution. As a symbol of suffering, the cross continues to have meaning within the Catholic tradition.

Although the cross as a symbol of suffering has a strong tradition within Catholicism, it is seldom expressed in Protestant circles. As a symbol of suffering, the cross is not intended to lead one to worship pain or suffering. Rather, this symbol of the cross reminds us that if we seek to experience life to the fullest, we must be willing to embrace suffering. It is a paradox in life that as we embrace our suffering, we find a liberation or resurrection in spirit. We cannot escape suffering in this life. Instead of attempting to flee from suffering, the cross can stand as a symbol inviting us to embrace our suffering with creativity and the promise of later resurrection of spirit. This is what is meant by bearing one's cross. When we are able to flow with suffering, we move with it and through it. The contemporary German theologian Jürgen Moltmann would argue that it is only in suffering that we truly experience that which we call God.

The psychologist Rollo May says that our best work comes in the painful valleys and our growing is always born in pain and suffering. It was Aristotle who said, "Pain is a passion of the soul." Both of these quotes allude to a theology and symbolism of the cross that encourages one to embrace suffering, not as religious masochists, but in the faith that suffering embraced brings eventual liberation and resurrection of individual spirit.

Lastly, the cross is a reminder of our Christian heritage and Christian roots. The circle and off-center cross was a popular symbol for Universalists from the 1940s until the Universalist and Unitarian marriage in 1961. Many Universalist heritage churches continue to use the symbol of the circle and off-center cross. The cross was placed to one side of the circle to acknowledge the Christian heritage of the Universalist faith and to stress that no one symbol, form, or expression was entitled to the central place as the symbol or vehicle for the Universalist spirit. Within this Universalist circle there is room for all of humanity's expressions and symbols of faith.

Symbol of life and immortality, symbolic invitation to embrace our suffering, and/or reminder of our Christian heritage—the Easter cross can have meaning for Universalists. May we find some relevant and new meaning in a very ancient symbol, the cross, this Easter holiday.

10

What Does Prison Life Have in Common with the First Christmas?

(A Christmas Sermon Delivered to an Inmate Congregation)

Luke 2:1–7; 22:14–20

LIBERATION THEOLOGY SPEAKS TO the suffering of oppressed people. One of the more prominent of the liberation theologians is the German Jürgen Moltmann. In his book *The Church in the Power of the Spirit*, he suggests that the true church, which is the risen Christ, is only present in the midst of suffering. He says to go where people suffer and there you will find Christ. He proclaims that a church that is not somehow connected to the suffering of people is not the true church. The New Testament, like the Old Testament, is a chronicle of a suffering people, the people of Christ, and the suffering savior.

Although Christmas is celebrated as the birth of Jesus, little of the Christmas festivities have much to do with Jesus. Much of the Christmas holidays are marked by festive decorations, colorful lights, lovely Christmas trees, and family get-togethers. For folks who are separated from family and friends at this time of year, the festivity of this season is almost a punishment. When others appear to have a joy that you are lacking, it only increases your own feelings of isolation and depression. I question whether Santa Clauses, lighted Christmas trees, and other Christmas decorations have any place within a prison. Such Christmas decorations stand only to remind us of where we are. We are away from our homes. We are not with our families. And there is not much festive about being in a prison during the Christmas season. I want to tell you that it is OK if you're not feeling very festive about Christmas. And I want to suggest to you that the best way to get through this holiday season is to ignore the Christmas festivities and instead focus upon the one whose birth we celebrate.

You know, Jesus had much more in common with you than he has with the festivities of this holiday. Much of the life of Jesus was a life of suffering. We have come to glorify nativity scenes depicting Jesus' birth. The manger scenes look so cozy and warm. We forget that the manger was a feed trough in a smelly and cold stable. Cow, sheep, goat, and camel manure probably covered the dirt floor of the stable. Think how lonely and desperate Mary and Joseph were that night. They were away from family in a strange city. They were without friends. Here they faced the humiliation of giving birth to a child in a smelly and cold stable. Their situation was more akin to the plight of many homeless families trying to make it from day to day in cities all across this nation.

The first Christmas Eve was no doubt a very depressing time for Joseph and Mary. There was nothing festive about being turned away from every inn in Bethlehem. There was nothing festive about spending a cold December night in an animal stable littered with animal waste. And what a rude entry into this world for the baby Jesus! His actual birth took place on a cold animal feeding trough. And the first smell that the baby Jesus encountered was not frankincense! The first smell was probably the stench of animal manure.

Those of you who are fighting back feelings of despair this holiday season are more akin to Mary and Joseph in what they were feeling than are those who are caught up in the festivities of this season.

Nor was there much festivity during the course of Jesus' life. Much of Jesus' ministry involved sharing in the suffering of others, with the poor and the outcast and with the disciples and their families and friends. In the end, Jesus suffered agony in the garden of Gethsemane and the desolation of the cross.

Later this spring we will observe Palm Sunday. This was when Jesus made his triumphant approach to Jerusalem. Folks lined the streets to greet him. According to Matthew, fresh-cut palm leaves were placed on the road to honor Jesus. Five days later, Jesus was crucified. You have to wonder, where were all those folks who honored Jesus, when after Jesus was arrested Pilate asked the crowd whether to release Barabbas or release Jesus. According to Luke, the whole crowd shouted, Kill Jesus and set Barabbas free! How quickly some people change. Maybe you can relate to what happened to Jesus this week. Some friends that you thought were friends before you became an inmate are no longer to be heard from. They deserted you just as quickly as did the folks who lined the streets to greet Jesus on that original Palm Sunday.

In the Gospel's account of Jesus, we find him to be one with human sensitivity beyond the endowment of anyone before or since. Rejection and rebuff by friends and relatives must have cut through with an uncommon painfulness. And that excruciating experience of being "odd," of having no one who understands, must have been magnified horribly in his lonely encounters with disciples and adversaries.

And then the Garden of Gethsemane! If one has ever suffered the throat-drying fear and panic of mental anguish, then the bloody sweat of Christ's Gethsemane will have special meaning.

But a Christian never suffers alone. A sufferer's pain is an invisible handclasp with all those who make up Christ's own body. And what is Christ's body? It is the church. A Christian suffering today, whether in slums or a mental hospital or a cancer ward or a prison or a home for the aged—for all Christians there is a mysterious link with all others who have been fused to Christ in martyrdom though the ages. Their suffering—and the Christ's suffering—become one and the same.

Suffering, as indicated in all of the Passion readings, is a distressful experience, but, again, it need not be a solo experience. It is a suffering that can be shared by fellow sufferers, thereby lightening the load for all, as the people of the Bible exemplify.

All people suffer. Even those who experience relatively minor suffering in their own lives are constantly confronted with the suffering of others—within families, among acquaintances, or even in distant places such as Africa, Asia, Eastern Europe, and the Middle East.

Suffering takes many forms: physical pain, frustrated hopes, depression, isolation, loneliness, grief, spiritual crisis, and more. Human efforts to explain with satisfaction all experiences of suffering are doomed to frustration. Answers may be found that are partially satisfying, that may work in some cases, or that may provide some help for the need to find meaning, but no matter how hard one tries, unanswered questions remain. At some point, one is finally confronted with the necessity of giving up the intellectual search and leaving the unknown in the care of God. There is much we will never know nor understand regarding the spiritual life.

A Psalm that I often read at funeral services is Psalm 90. Psalm 90 describes human life and human suffering. I won't read the entire psalm this morning, but I would like to share with you verse 10. The Psalmist writes, "Seventy years is all we have . . . eighty years, if we are strong; yet all they bring us is trouble and suffering; life is soon over, and we are gone."

Life consists of a lot of suffering, but one thing we do know, however, and that is that the pain of suffering can be alleviated through sharing. Suffering usually can be endured when a fellow sufferer goes through the experience with another. Jesus longed for that in his suffering, calling out to God, and even asking of his disciples, "Could you not wait with me one hour?"

Jesus saw the need of shared suffering, and we are called to follow his example in relieving the suffering of others and helping them bear their suffering patiently. Christians are to share in one another's sufferings and in the suffering of Christ. Paul identified the suffering community so closely with Christ's body that he could write in Galatians 2:20, "I have been crucified with Christ; it is no longer I who live, but Christ who lives in me."

There are difficult conditions or circumstances in life. Being in prison during the Christmas season is a particularly difficult experience for most inmates. But may you find comfort in the knowledge that your own suffering is more akin to the suffering of Jesus than any of the festivities and partying that will take place outside these prison fences. And know that despite the illusion of Christmas festivities, there are many people outside these prison fences suffering this holiday season as you are suffering. No one escapes suffering, although some people seem to get larger shares than others. But whatever the pain, the anxiety, the desolation, or the suffering, it is reassuring to know that God—perhaps through our Christian community—will embrace us as surely as Mary's arms enfolding the baby Jesus brought some comfort and peace in a cold and smelly stable.

We find strength for our shared suffering through sharing the suffering of Jesus. And this is what sharing the cross is about. As Christians participate in the suffering of Jesus, they can then share in the sufferings of others.

May we reach out in love to those around us who suffer this Christmas season, and may we be receptive to those expressions of love from those who would seek to share with us our own suffering. This is what it means for a church community to be the body of Christ.

Jesus said that we were to celebrate the Last Supper or Holy Communion in remembrance of him. What better way to share our suffering with one another and to experience God's presence than to observe Holy Communion this Christmas Eve. I invite you to join with us for this historic sacrament.

Delivered to inmates at Evans Correctional Institution, Bennettsville, South Carolina, on December 24, 1994. Evans is a maximum-security prison within the South Carolina Department of Corrections.

11

A Grateful Heart

Luke 17:11–19

IN THE SCRIPTURE READING from Luke, we find a story involving gratitude and the lack of gratitude. Ten men with leprosy are healed, but
only one returns to thank Jesus for his healing. What happened to the
other nine? Were the other nine ungrateful? I doubt it. Surely, all ten must
have been very happy for being cured from their disease. But nine of the
ten didn't make the effort to return and give a personal word of thanks.

I've come to believe that there is some universal truth in this scripture. It is my experience that the person who takes the time to express
gratitude by a letter, phone call, or an e-mail message is the exception
rather than the rule. I imagine that many of you have found the same to
be true. Most Christmas, birthday, and other special occasion gifts that I
mail to cousins, brothers, nieces, and nephews go unanswered. The same
is true for many friends. Actually, I have been amazed at how few people
there are who actually express thanks for gifts received. This sometimes
leads to awkward and embarrassing situations. You sometimes wonder
if the gift was received—especially if you later see this person and still
there is no mention of the gift. If I now make a monetary gift to a family
member or friend, I always write a check. At least I can check with my
bank to see if the check was cashed!

This past summer, I made a group photo of all the members of the
Quaker retreat I attended. At the group's request, I made copies of the
group photo and mailed copies to every group member along with a short
note. Of the nine photos and notes mailed, only one person has written

me back to say "thanks." I have discussed this phenomenon with a few of my friends who do stay in touch and who send thank you notes, and they tell me that their experiences are similar. It seems most people do not express gratitude if it requires special effort to do so. Or perhaps, we lose our feeling of gratitude as time passes.

The famous Scottish surgeon Joseph Lister was called upon to take care of a rich lord who had a fish bone stuck in his throat. The great doctor skillfully extracted the fish bone. In a rush of gratitude, the lord asked what he owed. Lister replied, "My lord, suppose we settle for half of what you were willing to give me while the bone was still stuck in your throat."

Of course, I guess there are a few occasions in life when we receive something for which we thought we would be grateful, but later regretted the gift. I suppose this goes with the saying "Be careful what you pray for because you just might get it." A collection of children's letters to Santa Claus includes the following short note: "Dear Santa Claus: Last Christmas I asked you for a baby brother. This Christmas I want you to take him back. Love, Susan."

Will Rogers, the great American humorist, said, "In the days of its founders, Americans were willing to give thanks for mighty little, for mighty little was all they expected. But now neither government nor nature can give enough but what we think it is too little. In the fall of the year, if the founders could gather a few pumpkins, some potatoes, and some corn for the winter, they were in a thanking mood. But now if we can't gather in a new car, a new radio, a new tuxedo, and some government relief, we feel like the world is against us."

Well, as we approach this Thanksgiving holiday, I want to encourage you to reflect upon this expression of appreciation that we call gratitude. Let us recall the people, the events, the blessings, and the gifts of the past year that have given us feelings of gratitude. How often did we go out of our way to express our gratitude? Have we forgotten much of our gratitude of the past year? Let us take a few moments of silence now to recall the people, the events, the blessings, and the gifts that have enriched our lives during the past year.

In the film *Grand Canyon*, Mack is a corporate lawyer who is rescued from a gang of black toughs bent on robbing him one night when his car breaks down in a rough area of Los Angeles. His unlikely rescuer is another black man, Simon, a tough truck operator with a strong sense of commitment to his work. Simon manages to talk the gang leader out of his conquest. Mack thanks his benefactor and returns safely home. But the next day he looks up Simon and invites him to breakfast. A simple "thanks" isn't enough; he tells Simon how years before he was saved from stepping out into the path of a bus by a woman. She had merged into the crowd, and Mack had ever since wondered about her and regretted not being able to thank her for saving his life. He does not intend to let that happen again. The rest of the film shows how an unusual friendship grows out of this sense of gratitude.

Ed Spencer was in a similar position when he was a student at Northwestern University in Evanston, Illinois. Ed and his classmates heard an excursion boat had been capsized in a storm off the coast of Lake Michigan. The students rushed to the lake to pull out the survivors. Ed saved seventeen people himself.

Decades later Ed's story was being told to a large audience in Los Angeles when a gentleman stood up to announce that Edward Spencer was present in the audience. The speaker invited Spencer forward and asked him what his most memorable part of the rescue was. The audience grew silent when Spencer said, "Of the seventeen people I saved, not one ever thanked me."

Just how transforming a grateful heart can be is well shown in the famous scene "The Bishop's Candlesticks" in *Les Miserables*. No one will give shelter to the itinerant Jean Valjean because of his yellow passport, branding him as an ex-convict. But an elderly clergyman takes him in, feeds him on his best silver plate, and bids him good night. Tormented by his nightmares of brutal treatment while a prisoner, Valjean awakens and steals the bishop's silver. Caught by the police, he is brought back to the bishop. To everyone's surprise the clergyman says that the plate was a gift, and he chides Valjean for leaving behind the two silver candlesticks. When the two are alone the bishop reaches the soul of Valjean and urges him, in effect, "to go and do likewise." Valjean thereafter becomes an agent of grace, bringing help and hope to all whom he meets, even while being hounded by Javert, a police inspector.

Grateful people do not count their blessings. They share them and don't keep count. People who are divided, suspicious, and jealous of one another, people who must demand and wrest a place for themselves, people who withhold a place from others—such people do keep accounts, must keep accounts. And it's easy for gratitude to get lost in the ledger.

William Blake once said that "gratitude is heaven itself." I think there is much truth in Blake's comment. I have found that the most grateful people are also the happiest.

I encourage us, you and me, to seek and claim a grateful heart this Thanksgiving. Take some time to reflect and try and gain a true sense of appreciation for those people, events, gifts, and blessings that have come your way and enriched your life.

12

The Judas Principle

Acts 1:15–26

IN OUR SCRIPTURE FROM Acts we read of the betrayal and death of Judas, one of the original twelve disciples. Also in these words of scripture, verse 17, we are told that Judas had been numbered among the twelve and had been allotted to share in God's ministry. In verse 21 we are reminded that Judas, until the time of his betrayal of Jesus, had been an integral member of the disciple community. We are told in verse 21 that Judas had accompanied Jesus "all the time" during the ministry of Jesus.

We're not talking about a marginal disciple. If Judas was a member of a church, he would have been one of those members whom you could count on to be present whenever the church held an activity or a worship service.

We're told in the scripture reading that Judas had always been there. Judas had heard all the sermons that Jesus had ever preached. Judas had been an active participant in all the conversations that Jesus had had with his disciples. Judas had shared in the ministry of Jesus. And yet, in verse 25, we are told that Judas turned aside, to go to his own place.

After coming to know God through the ministry of Jesus . . .

After witnessing the words of truth as spoken by Jesus . . .

How could Judas have turned aside to go his own place?

Here we are left with a new truth, even after coming to find a spiritual path in one's life, there will be some individuals who seem destined to desert that path. And the greater truth might be that for all of us—regardless of how holy, loving, and spiritual we may seem to be—there remains, nonetheless, a tendency or temptation to go our own place. There remains within us a stubborn clinging to that which is irredeemable within each of us. This Judas principle can push any one of us to the worst possible scenario.

Many religious mystics tell us that the further along we are on our spiritual path, the greater is the degree to which we are apt to fall if we turn away from that path. If we seriously consider what these mystics are telling us, there could be a good argument for stating that Judas' awareness and knowledge of God had been greater than the other eleven disciples'—for the degree to which Judas fell was certainly of the greatest magnitude.

We must keep in mind that the Judas principle was not limited to the psyche of Judas. The Judas principle was very much present with each of the twelve disciples. For every one of the other eleven disciples, there was each day a tension between that which was irredeemable within them and that which was divine.

The decision to become a disciple of Jesus was not a one-time event. The decision to become a disciple was a daily event. Actually, it was more than a daily event; it was a constant state of decision.

So it is for each one of us. At every moment, the Judas principle is present within us. Within each one of us, at any moment, there is a tension between going our own way and going the way that reflects divine will.

I think we are in error if we think of Judas, from the very beginning, as being somehow or somewhat less than the other eleven disciples. What happened to Judas could have happened to any of the other eleven. What happened to Judas can happen to any one of us.

The call of God, the call to follow a spiritual path, is a decision that must be renewed each and every day. The analogy has been made between spirituality and awareness. As we become more spiritual, we become more aware. First and foremost, we become more aware of that which we call God:

- More aware of that which we call God in our thoughts
- More aware of that which we call God in the world around us
- More aware of that which we call God in our relationships with others
- More aware of that which we call God speaking to us from scripture readings

We also become less self-centered and more aware of the concerns, hurts, and struggles of others.

Becoming less spiritual corresponds with losing awareness. Falling away from one's spiritual path is like wearing tinted glasses and each day wearing a darker shade. And as the shades become darker and darker, we forget the brilliant sunlight and clarity of vision that was once ours to see. Where once we could see light, we now see only darkness. Yet some of us call the darkness light. In the darkness, it becomes more difficult to see our path. We stumble. We can lose our way. We become more attached to possessions, emotions, greed, and anger. We may make wrong decisions, and we can even fall, just as Judas fell.

Regardless of your faith yesterday or even today, each one of us has the potential to fall away from our own higher good—to fall away from that which we call God. And falling away from that which we call God and going our own way is usually not a radical event. Rather it is a gradual event, like putting on darker and darker sunglasses.

In the past couple of years some Americans have been amused and others dismayed by the revelations surrounding some of our more well known television evangelists. Many Christians have had their faith shaken by the reports of wrongdoing associated with these television preachers. However, if we take seriously our scripture reading from Acts, these events should strengthen our faith. Our scripture would lead us to expect that there will always be some ministers who will fall away from their spiritual calling, as well as other lay people who will do the same.

Perhaps some churches and denominations have put their ministers and preachers on pedestals that are too high. It is sometimes easier for folks to see Jesus' own twelve disciples as vulnerable human beings than it is for churches to see their own pastors that way.

This is in no way to imply that we should excuse sin among the clergy. Furthermore, it would seem to me that there should be a stricter accountability for those of us who are paid as church leaders. But the real danger for any one of us is if we begin thinking that we are beyond sin, regardless of what our role in the church may be. Self-righteousness can be just another pair of dark sunglasses—dark sunglasses by which our own pride and self-will are often mistaken for divine will. We must remember that as long as we live, we are subject to the Judas principle.

In Alcoholics Anonymous there is what is called the twenty-four-hour plan. When you join AA, you aren't required to say that you will never drink again. Instead you concentrate on keeping sober for just the current twenty-four hours. In AA you simply try to get through one day at a time without a drink. Perhaps it would be helpful if we as Universalists adopted a similar twenty-four-hour plan. A plan in which each day we begin that day with a short devotional, meditation, or prayer and make a conscious decision to live that day in a way that is in harmony with our faith journey.

The Judas principle is a possibility for any one of us. We need to watch for the Judas principle within ourselves. And in a loving and caring way we need to watch for the Judas principle within our brothers and sisters.

Jesus tells us to pray always. Perhaps this request is related to the Judas principle. Not that we should always be praying a verbal prayer, but that we need to be mindful of God and our spiritual path throughout the day.

The theme of this morning's sermon is the Judas principle. I hope you will leave this church today with the awareness that no one of us is beyond succumbing to the Judas principle. However, I want to conclude on a more positive note.

There is a flip side to the Judas principle. We might call it the Paul principle. Paul has frequently been called "the second founder of Christianity." Before Paul experienced his Damascus-road conversion, Paul was known as Saul of Tarsus. Saul had been heavily involved with the persecution of the early church. He was even present as an approving spectator at the stoning of Stephen. The Paul principle is that even in the individual who appears to be most irredeemable there is, nonetheless, the possibility of the best. We see the Paul principle operative in the great church father, St. Augustine. Prior to his conversion, Augustine was mostly known for his unruly passions. As a young man, we are told he was unable to give up the lusts of the flesh. In his book *Confessions* when Augustine looks back on his early adulthood, he writes that if he had a prayer at this promiscuous time in his life, his prayer would have been "Grant me chastity, but not yet."

Out of what may appear most irredeemable is found the possibility of the best. Even with Judas, had he not committed suicide out of his despair and guilt over betraying Jesus, I am sure that the Paul principle might have also occurred.

As we can never be so godly in our life as to be immune from sin and falling from God's grace, likewise, we can never be as hopeless and wretched as to be beyond the hope of redemption and the experience of grace.

13

Lao Tzu, Buddha, Jesus,
and a Ride Down Memory Lane

A COUPLE OF MONTHS ago, the training sergeant in my Raleigh, North Carolina, Army Reserve unit telephoned and asked me if I wanted to fly or drive to Hattiesburg, Mississippi, for the two-week residence phase of the U.S. Army Command and General Staff College. The sergeant said that there were no direct flights to Hattiesburg and that it would take eight hours to get there by plane due to having to change planes three times. The sergeant thought I could probably drive it in thirteen hours, plus the army would give me two days of extra pay should I decide to drive. I decided to drive and make my trip a semi-vacation. The inspiration for this morning's sermon came as a result of my two-day drive to Hattiesburg, Mississippi.

I drove to Barnwell, South Carolina, Thursday evening, June 8, and spent the night with my mother and stepfather. Friday morning I began my two-day drive to Mississippi. First I visited my youngest brother and his family in Aiken, South Carolina. In Augusta, Georgia, I stopped by a nursing home to visit an uncle. He is an uncle with whom I spent a great deal of time with while growing up. He suffered a stroke two years ago and has been bedridden ever since. Although he remains very alert, he has a difficult time speaking. I was barely able to understand anything he tried to tell me. His inability to communicate was frustrating for him and he cried several times during his attempts to converse with me. It was painful for me to see him suffer, and I am sure it was painful for him to no longer have the freedom to speak.

After leaving the nursing home, I continued down Interstate 20 until I came to the Thomson, Georgia, exit. I had decided to retrace an old bicycle trip that I once made across Georgia in 1972. The motel where I spent my first night was the Cotton Patch motel in Thomson. As I drove through the small town of Thomson, nothing looked as I had remembered the place. I was unable to find the Cotton Patch motel anywhere. A man at a local gas station told me that the Cotton Patch motel had been torn down several years ago in order to build a new hospital.

I continued to follow my old bicycle route. I drove through Warrenton, Sparta, Milledgeville, Gray, and Warm Springs, Georgia. There were places along the way where the scenery was just as I had remembered it, but in most of the towns, everything seemed different. Roads that had been two lanes were now four lanes. Shopping malls had replaced many of the country stores. At Warm Springs, I departed from my route to head southwest to Columbus, Georgia. I was to spend the evening with my former seminary roommate, who is now minister of a United Methodist Church in Phenix City, Alabama, just across the state line from Columbus.

My seminary classmate and I shared a room in the upstairs of a house in which all the rooms were rented to seminary students at Emory University. Actually, he and I were only part-time roommates. He was married at the time and was serving a student pastorate in Alabama along with completing his theological studies at Emory. His wife and three young daughters lived in the parsonage while he would drive to Atlanta every Monday night, take classes on Tuesday, Wednesday, and Thursday, and then he was usually back on the road to Alabama Thursday night. Maybe that is why we got along so well. We were only together three nights a week. He and I finished Emory in 1976 and have continued to stay in touch by phone and letter.

Last spring a year ago, he stopped by my home in Clio, South Carolina, while en route to a United Methodist ministers' school being held in Myrtle Beach. It was the first time that we had seen one another in over ten years. It was then that he told me that he and his wife were having serious marital problems and that they would probably separate later that summer. They did separate and their divorce was final last fall. This has been a difficult year for my seminary friend. He has lost over sixty pounds in the past two years and he hasn't been dieting. He says he just doesn't have any appetite. He is presently dating a woman he recently met, but he isn't sure if this new relationship will lead anywhere. He still loves his wife very much. We stayed up until after midnight talking. We shared a few laughs about old times, but overall, it was a bittersweet visit. Divorce is a painful event. It affects so many people. As much as my seminary classmate grieves his marriage of twenty-three years ending, he also grieves the impact the divorce has had on his children. One daughter rarely visits or calls. He is struggling with his own sense of shame and failure, and he is struggling with whether or not to remain in the parish ministry.

After breakfast, I headed west toward Montgomery. Along Interstate 85 about thirty miles east of Montgomery, a black Nissan began honking its horn at me. It pulled alongside me and a woman motioned for me to pull over. I didn't recognize the woman and I wasn't about to pull over. But then the car pulled in front of me and the driver stuck his head out of the window just enough for me to recognize him. It was Anibal Cruz and his family. I last saw Anibal in 1989. He and I both served as army chaplains at Fort Jackson. The last time that I saw Anibal he was on his way for a three-year tour of duty in Puerto Rico. Anibal said that my dirty Nissan pick-up was one of a kind, and when he spotted it he knew it must be me. Here's just another reason why it is good to keep the same vehicle a long time. People recognize you. So on the side of Interstate 85, Anibal and I visited for about twenty minutes as other cars and trucks zoomed by us. We exchanged addresses and telephone numbers. I gave him a copy of the *Universalist Herald*, and we both swore that we would stay in touch in the future.

The shortest route to Hattiesburg would have been to proceed west from Montgomery, but I had already decided that I wanted to drive south through Brewton, Alabama. Brewton was where I had my first parish ministry experience. I was the associate minister at the Universalist Church in Brewton from 1976 to 1978. I had not been back to Brewton since 1978. I don't feel particularly proud about my time in Brewton. I was a young twenty-three-year-old when I accepted the position at the church. It had been less than a year since I made the switch from United Methodist to Unitarian Universalist when I began my ministry in Brewton. I was more into what I didn't believe than articulating what I did believe. At that time in my life, I considered Universalism the old-fashioned half of Unitarian Universalism. I preferred to call myself Unitarian or UU. I drove a 400 Kawasaki motorcycle and had a beard and long hair. I was not very discreet in either my partying or my dating during those two years. I was probably remembered more for my colorfulness than my ministerial or pastoral style.

Well, I had stayed in touch with a couple of people in Brewton until 1981, but had not heard from anyone since that time. The Universalist Church in Brewton stopped holding worship services in 1980 following the deaths of the church's two patriarchs. As I drove into Brewton, I felt like I had entered the Twilight Zone. Some places looked just as I had remembered them. Other places looked entirely different. After driving around town for thirty minutes or so, I decided that I just had to see if there was still someone there who I might still know. I stopped by the hospital and borrowed the local telephone book in the hospital waiting room. As I searched the pages, name after name was missing. Whether they had moved or died, I did not know.

Finally, I found the name of the widow of a prominent member of the church. Without first calling, I drove to her home. I rang her doorbell and after a few minutes, she appeared at the door. Although I recognized her, she did not recognize me. It took her a few minutes to recall who I was. After she realized who I was, she invited me into her home. We visited for thirty minutes or so. She shared with me news of her family. I was struck by how much tragedy and sorrow she had experienced in the past seventeen years. She told me of the deaths of several members of her family, including a son-in-law who was struck by lightening and a granddaughter who was killed in an auto accident. There had been several other serious accidents and illnesses. One daughter-in-law that I remember as being very vivacious was near death with Lupus disease. Another child had divorced. Practically every member of the congregation at the Universalist Church had since died.

I left her home struck by the degree of sorrow and suffering that a family can experience over a seventeen-year period. Maybe her story is not unique. I thought about my own family and all that has happened in the past seventeen years. When we look over a seventeen-year period, can we not find similar stories of sorrow and suffering?

As I was leaving Brewton, I made an impulsive decision to head south through Jay, Florida. Jay is only fifteen miles south of Brewton. My seminary roommate now living in Phenix City, Alabama, had told me that a fellow housemate from our time at Emory was now the new minister of the United Methodist Church in Jay. In fact, I was told that this was his first week in his new parish.

When I arrived at the church, I could see folks were gathering for a wedding. I parked my Nissan truck and walked over to the parsonage. After ringing the doorbell, my former seminary housemate came to the door. Jim looked pretty much like I remembered him from seminary, but Jim obviously did not recognize me. When I realized Jim did not know who I was, I could not resist playing a practical joke. I asked Jim why he was not over at the church for the wedding.

Jim responded, "I'm not performing the wedding. The previous minister of the church is doing the wedding."

I responded, "No, you are supposed to do the wedding. I was sent over here to see why you are not at the church."

"No, there must be a misunderstanding. I am sure the previous minister is handling the wedding. I just moved to Jay last week," retorted Jim.

"Look preacher," I said. "My mother has been a member of Jay United Methodist Church for over fifty years. She says you are supposed to do this wedding and she is not going to like it if you refuse to handle it."

"There must be a mistake, but I will get over to the church just as soon as I change my clothes and get my pulpit robe," Jim responded looking a bit nervous.

At this point I could not help but start laughing. Jim looked puzzled by my laughter.

"Jim, I said. "Don't you recognize who I am?"

"Well, the voice sounds a little familiar but I don't recognize your face," Jim replied.

"Jim, this is Vernon Chandler. We shared the upstairs of a house at Emory in 1974 through 1976. Have I changed that much over the past twenty years?" I asked.

"Vernon! Yes, that is you! I didn't recognize you without the long hair and beard." Jim added, "I knew I wasn't supposed to do that wedding. You really had me going."

Jim invited me into the parsonage and we visited for about thirty minutes. We shared with one another some of our significant highlights of the past twenty or so years.

From Jay, Florida, I drove back across the state line and headed to Atmore, Alabama. I had to see the state prisons located outside Atmore. I had worked at Fountain and Holman state prisons as a part-time mental health counselor while serving as the associate minister at the Universalist Church in Brewton. Driving by the prison felt surprisingly good. The prison looked about like I remembered it. The inmates in the yard looked like the inmates walking the yard at Evans Correctional Institution near Bennettsville, South Carolina, where I now work as a chaplain. Momentarily, I thought about all the inmates at Evans with whom I now have relationships and just how important relationships are in life. Our relationships with one another are really the most important and meaningful aspect of human life. Too often, we learn this truth too late in life.

During the remainder of my drive to Mississippi, I reflected upon the emotional roller coaster of the past two days. I decided that there were three truths that I had confirmed during my two-day journey down memory lane. Each truth is best expressed by different religious traditions. The first truth that was made painfully aware to me was the truth of change. All life and creation is in constant change. Yet most of us resist change or deny change. Perhaps Lao Tzu, the founder of Taoism, best expressed this truth. He wrote, "Nature is not benevolent; with ruthless indifference she makes all things serve their purposes, like the straw dogs we use at sacrifices. What is contrary to the Tao soon perishes." Elsewhere he writes, "All things come into existence, and thence we see them return. Look at the things that have been flourishing; each goes back to its origin." Taoism teaches that there is a natural movement and flow to creation. In observing this natural movement, we witness change. Change is constant. We may not notice change over one day or one week. But revisit someone or someplace after an absence of a few years, and the change is pronounced.

From *Great Occasions*, edited by Carl Seaburg, is a reading by Robert T. Weston that I often use at funerals and memorial services. Weston's reading expresses well this truth about change. It goes like this:

> I planted a ripe seed, and it split, and where it had been, a green sprout appeared; but the seed disintegrated. The green sprout grew, a thing of beauty, sent down roots, sent out leaves, budded, flowered, bore fruit, decayed and was itself a withered thing. I could not even keep the ripe seed. Each in its time had its own peculiar beauty. All things change; nothing remains the same. So, each in its time, each life in its every moment—the baby, the child, the youth, the lover, the parent, the aged—is at its ultimate state in each moment and passes on. Pluck this moment as you would a precious flower; share it as if it were love, and let it go. Beauty and wonder lie all about you even now; they too, even as you, are never final, but always in process of being and becoming. Take, then, each moment as the perfect gift of life, knowing that you shall no more be able to hold it as it is than what is already past. Even as you let go, another and yet different moment comes.

Change was the first truth that I had driven home to me during my two-day trip down memory lane. I had witnessed so much change.

The second truth that I gleaned from my two-day trip was that of human suffering. There are moments of joy in human existence, but most of human life is suffering. All people suffer. Even those who experience relatively minor suffering in their own lives are constantly confronted with the suffering of others—within families, among acquaintances, or even in distant places. Suffering takes many forms: physical pain, frustrated hopes, depression, isolation, loneliness, grief, anxiety, and spiritual crisis. Another reading that I often use in funerals and memorial services is Psalm 90. The following is an adaptation by Emil Weitzner of this psalm as found in *Great Occasions*.

> Man is brought to the dust; to dust must man return. A thousand years are as a day that has passed as a watch in the night. Men are consigned to sleep; like grass, we are fresh in the morning, in the morning we sprout, blossom forth; in the evening we wither and fade. Our days decline and end as a sigh; Destined for seventy, with strength for eighty, most of them toil and travail, soon they pass as we fail. Let us, then, value our days, hallowing each with grace as a trust bestowed upon men, acquiring a heart full of wisdom and love for the living of earth. Through all the days though we suffer and all the years though we sorrow, rejoice and be glad always, for the precious gift give thanks: Live for the good each day.

Although all of the major religions of the world acknowledge human suffering, it is the Buddha who speaks most eloquently to this truth. The Buddha taught this as the first of his four holy truths. He said that all mortal existence is characterized by suffering. There are times in life, even long periods, when one is unaware of this characteristic, but ultimately it will assert itself and one will experience the bitter sense that things are not what they should be, nor as one could wish them to be. The Buddha taught that the more refined the sensibilities, the greater is the awareness of this basis characteristic in all mortal existence. The truth of human suffering is the basis of Buddhism. The other three holy truths relate to the cause of much of human suffering, and the eightfold path addresses eight precepts or behaviors that will result in less human suffering. But the first holy truth and the basis of Buddhism is the recognition of human suffering. The reality of human suffering was the second truth that I was made aware of during my two-day trip down memory lane.

The third truth that was made real to me during my two-day journey was that of the joy and beauty of love and relationships. The high points of my journey were those times when I connected with other people, that is, visiting with my brother and his family; visiting my uncle in the nursing home; spending the night with my former seminary roommate; being pulled over on the interstate by an army chaplain friend; visiting the elderly woman in Brewton, Alabama; visiting my former housemate in Jay, Florida; worshipping and renewing some old friendships at Our Home Universalist Church in Ellisville, Mississippi, during my free weekend from army classes; and even driving by the state prisons near Atmore, Alabama, and thinking of several of my inmate friends back in South Carolina.

It was Jesus of Nazareth who taught us this important truth. There is much unhealthy religiosity and downright idolatry associated with what is often preached as Christianity today, but in the lifestyle and teachings of Jesus of Nazareth we find love as the essence of his message. Church means community. A community is a body of people who relate to one another with compassion and love. The salvation that we receive from being involved with church is not due to belief or conversion. It is our relationships with one another that save us. Church is not church unless it is community. Loving relationships are what gives us the strength, the purpose, the meaning, and the joy of living despite the suffering and sorrows of life. We need one another. And our greatest joy comes not from acquiring but from giving—giving kindness and giving love to one another. This I believe was the heart of the message of Jesus. Perhaps this truth is best expressed in a selection of scripture found in John 13. Here Jesus says: "I give you a new command, 'Love one another.' Just as I have loved you, so you should love one another. By this everyone will recognize that you are my disciples if you love one another."

These were the three truths that I found confirmed in my two-day trip to Mississippi. I feel like Lao Tzu, Buddha, and Jesus were all three talking to me as I made my journey. Each truth is important. To deny change and human suffering will only increase our suffering. Love makes life bearable.

May we practice the religion of Jesus. May we affirm with love our human relationships with one another. This is the only way we're going to be able to survive the other truths of change and suffering that will continue to be a part of our life and living.

14

The Brevity of Life

How can you be so sure about your life? It is nothing more than mist that appears for only a little while before it disappears. (James 4:14)

IF YOU DIED TODAY would the world be any worse off without you? Does your life make any difference in the world? Would you be missed? The New Testament writer James raises such questions when he asks: "What is your life?" and then immediately adds that we will be mist. "For you are nothing more than mist," James writes, "that appears for only a little while before it disappears."

Rather deflating, isn't it—that your life is nothing but a mist that vanishes into thin air? But that's what James is doing, deflating the egos of those who are boastful and arrogant, who think their lives are one big splash, one colossal thunderstorm, while they are nothing more than mist, a vanishing vapor—short lived and of little consequence.

There are numerous activities and events that can have the effect of deflating our egos as does this passage from James. An activity that has a way of deflating my own ego is that of going out of doors on a clear night and observing the stars overhead. And now that I am back in the country, away from city lights, looking at the sky on a clear night is even more awesome and spectacular. I may get caught up into my work, family responsibilities, finances, the daily news, or whatever, and then go out, and as I view the millions of stars overhead, I am reminded of the vastness of this universe and of my own limited time here. And I find that the concerns of my ego are often deflated. This is especially true as I consider just how vast the universe actually is.

I want to give you a short astronomy course this morning that I want you to remember the next time you look up at the stars at night. I doubt that anyone in this congregation has actually seen an accurate scale model of our solar system. Diagrams in science books and models at science fairs are far from accurate as scale models. According to Neil McAleer in *The Cosmic Mind-Boggling Book*, a true scale model would look like this: If the Sun were represented by a yellow beach ball with a two-foot diameter, the Earth would be the size of a garden pea 215 feet away. Mars would also be about the size of a garden pea and would be about 125 feet beyond the pea-sized earth. Jupiter would be the size of a large orange 1,056 feet away. And the farthermost planet from the sun, Pluto, would be the size of a BB just under two miles away from the beach-ball size sun.

Now this illustration only involves the sun and nine planets. On any given night chances are that only one or two of the bright specks in the sky are one of the planets. Almost all of the specks of light we call stars are from outside our solar system. Now if you take this scale model of our solar system that I just described and shrink this scale model to a size that could fit into a coffee cup and take this coffee-cup size solar system and place it in our Milky Way galaxy using the same scale, the Milky Way galaxy would be the size of North America.

The Milky Way galaxy is only one of an estimated 100 billion galaxies in the universe. Many of what you think are stars at night are actually other galaxies, but they are so far away that they appear as a single star. However, if you take the North-America-size Milky Way galaxy with our solar system the size of a coffee cup and then reduce our galaxy to the size of a one ounce piece of steel, the other remaining galaxies would equal 100,000 tons of the same steel.

Maybe this has been too much astronomy for a Sunday morning, but I assure you that if the next time you look at the sky on a starry night, you begin pondering the actual distances involved with those stars, it does have a way of bringing humility and deflating the ego.

James asks, "How can you be so sure about your life? It is nothing more than mist that appears for only a little while before it disappears."

The context for these remarks from James is a situation where merchants plan and act as if God did not exist and as if they instead of God controlled life. James is addressing people who have shut spirituality out of their commercial lives, although they may be pious enough in church and at home. James declares that no part of life is outside the rule of God and that commercial independence is evil and leads one to arrogance and boastfulness and an attitude that one can go it alone and be successful. James brings such boasters down to earth by reminding them that they are mist, nothing but steam, and even that is not for long.

J. Richard Kennedy is the author of a novel entitled *Short Term*. It is the story of a forty-two-year-old businessman named Ken Preston. Ken is "successful" in the business sense of that word. Like the businessmen in the Epistle of James, he can "go into such and such a town and spend a year there and trade and get gain." He has all the money he needs. He has a splendid house and drives a Jaguar. He has all the trappings of affluence. But Ken is not a happy man. He lives with a low-grade depression. Like the men in the Bible, he tries to compensate by glorying in his material success, boasting of his accumulations. But it doesn't work for him either. At one point in the story he says that he feels like a person who is shouting: Rah! Rah! Rah! for absolutely no reason at all. Another time he says that he feels like a "Quarterback on a timeless Monday morning who keeps seeing the scoreboard and the big zero."

Kennedy's story echoes and affirms what the biblical writer James stated years ago. It's a familiar one to us today—business executives, overly ambitious men and women of many different careers and vocations, whose life is their work, who forget to go home, and when home who are spiritually absent from that which they call home.

Anyone can fall victim to formulating life into false and graven idols: rewards, prizes, degrees, recognition, money, promotion, titles. Now, none of this is in and of itself wrong. In fact it is good and healthy in life to have goals that include rewards, prizes, education, recognition, money, promotion, and titles. But if the desire for these things is formulating life into false and graven idols, then they are all attempts to rise above mist and pretend to be more than we are or should be.

Not only are we as a mist, but James adds that we only appear for a little time and then we vanish. Life is short, and the older we become; the more we realize just how short a human life is.

My Dad bought an 8mm movie camera in 1958 for the purpose of capturing family vacations, Christmases, birthdays, reunions, and other special events in our family life. The last time the camera was used was in 1973. The little movie reels remained in a box since that time. Two Christmases ago, I brought the hundred or so small reels to a camera shop and had the movies transferred to a video cassette in chronological order and had copies made as Christmas gifts for my two younger brothers. It only took about three and a half hours to cover the entire fifteen-year span. The first time that I viewed the entire video and witnessed our progressive aging through the various family vacations and Christmases, I was reminded of the brevity of human life. Also, I realized that I am now older than my Dad was when he bought the camera in 1958.

Chaim Potok, in his book *The Chosen*, writes that human beings do not live forever. We live less than the time it takes to blink an eye, if we measure our lives against eternity. So it may be asked what value there is to a human life. There is so much pain in the world. What does it mean to have to suffer so much if our lives are nothing more than the blink of an eye?

Potok writes that he learned a long time ago that a blink of an eye in itself is nothing. But the eye that blinks, *that* is something. A span of life is nothing. But the person who lives that span, *he* or *she* is something. He or she can fill that tiny span with meaning, so its quality is immeasurable, though its quantity may be insignificant.

Oftentimes, all of the endeavors, ambitions, worldly goals, and the living of our lives as though we would be on this earth forever can be vain attempts to fool ourselves into believing that we are more than mist. But not only that, in our franticness, we also push that which we call God and our spirituality aside.

Where is that which we call God in our life this morning?

What is the true meaning of our life this morning?

What is the state of our spirituality this morning?

Thomas Keir writes that on the western seaboard of Scotland, where the sea stretches long arms inland, the sound of the sea is constant, and if one is not aware of it, it is because it is always there, a kind of atmosphere. One may hear the lowing of the cattle, the cry of a mother calling her child, the ring of a spade striking rock. But only in moments of exquisite awareness does one consciously hear the unceasing sea and the winds. It is the very keynote of all sounds, the unremitting background music of everyday life, and for that reason not consciously noted.

It may be somewhat like that with the sense of God. People are attracted to the exotic in life, the excitement of business and commerce, stocks and bonds, real estate, and you can add countless items to this list—but the problem is that our spirituality often gets pushed into the background.

This is the point the Epistle of James makes. Business and commerce, the desire for promotion, the goal of someday being at the top of your career ladder, educational degrees, a nice house—these are not in and of itself evil; these can be good goals; but it is the inordinate attraction to them and the artificial self-importance we feel from them that is sin, because our spiritual life is pushed aside. Loving and caring relationships are pushed aside.

Whatever we do with our short life on Earth, we must realize that the mystery we call God must be joined to it in order for meaning and fulfillment to be realized. No vocation or honor or bank account or brokerage account can stand alone. One of the basic lessons of our short span of life is to know that that which we call God must be a part of whatever we do.

As you depart the church later today, I ask that you reflect on this scripture passage from James.

"How can you be so sure about your life? It is nothing more than mist that appears for only a little while before it disappears."

Think about your own journey through life.

What is the meaning and purpose of your life?

What do you hope to accomplish during the remainder of your life?

Is that which we call God a conscious aspect of your life's journey?

15

Living with Our Wounds: An Easter Sermon

Mark 15:22–37

O N EASTER SUNDAY, IT is customary for this congregation to honor Jesus. This is the day that we observe our annual communion service. On this day, we pay tribute to Jesus of Nazareth. From our *Beacon Song and Service Book*, there is a beautiful responsive reading that expresses the Universalist view of Jesus. It goes like this:

> We hold in reverence the name of Jesus of Nazareth, who has shown us how to live in fellowship, one with another. He taught us to know God as our Father and to love him with all our hearts. He taught the law of brotherhood . . . to love our neighbors as ourselves. He taught the law of mercy . . . to love our enemies and to return good for evil. He loved the beauty of nature, and drew sacred lessons from the birds and flowers, the sunshine and the rain. He loved little children, and laid his hands on them in blessing. He loved the poor and humble, and was a friend to the friendless. He came not to be served, but to serve; he was gentle and patient, but strong to resist evil. He taught that religion is not in word or form, but in kindly thought and generous deed. His trust was in God and in the unseen things which abide.

These are beautiful words in our responsive reading, but these words neglect another aspect of Jesus. Jesus was one who knew the meaning of suffering. Jesus knew the suffering of being misunderstood by his disciples. Jesus knew the suffering of being misunderstood by many of the people to whom he attempted to do his ministry. Jesus knew the suffering of being betrayed. Jesus knew the suffering of the night in Gethsemane when he told his disciples "I am so sad that I feel as if I am dying." Jesus experienced the sufferings of having what amounted to a mob choose him over Barabbas as the one they wanted executed. Jesus knew the suffering of being beaten with a whip. Jesus knew the suffering of having to carry his own cross to the site of the execution. Jesus knew the humiliation of having people spit on him as he made his way to Golgotha. And Jesus knew that suffering of the actual crucifixion. In biblical times, crucifixion was an awful way to die. It was a slow and painful death.

Wounded has joined a group of words and phrases that are overused to the point of having very little meaning. "I understand your pain," is a phrase the president of this country has become famous for saying. "I can't go back to church—it is too painful" is a phrase heard to describe parish conflict in many towns and cities.

These wounds, of lost expectations or hurt feelings, hardly compare to nails tacking hands to a wooden cross. But they do give us a window on woundedness. Even when we are hurt just a little, we still hurt a lot. It is hard to get over a wound. Scars, disfigurement, and limps all come to mind when we think of physical wounds. But there are also the inner wounds of fear, lost confidence, lost hope, and lost direction.

Some of us have been wounded in childhood by parents who could have loved us more but perhaps did not know how, or by not winning prizes we thought we should have won, or by dating relationships that did not work out, or by misplaced hopes.

Women who have been raped tell us that all they want back is "yesterday." How we handle our wounds is a key to who we are.

In the story of Jesus reappearing to his disciples, I think we can find an interesting analogy to the issue of wounds and woundedness. It was the doubting Thomas, sometimes called the Unitarian Universalist disciple, who questioned what the other disciples proclaimed. In the Gospel of John, Thomas is quoted as saying, "First, I must see the nail scars in his hands and touch them with my finger. I must put my hand where the spear went into his side. I won't believe unless I do this." And this apparition of Jesus or physically resurrected Jesus, as most Christians believe, says to Thomas, "Put your finger here and look at my hands! Put your hand into my side." Jesus used the wounds to prove that he was who he claimed to be. He did not go around his wounds, he used them.

Wounded people who survive their wounds do the same thing. Raped women find ways to go on with their heads held high. People whose parents fail them grow up around these failures. Scarred hearts in patients following cardiac arrests do the same: the heart beats around the scar and eventually through it.

The director of a group home was stabbed to death by one of the residents, one whom he had taken especially good care of over the years. The resident had secretly gone off his medication and his mental illness resurfaced. The family of the deceased director did an amazing thing: they visited the man who murdered their father and husband after the man was back on his medication. They befriended him. They handled the wounds the way Jesus handled his, by loving their enemy and being good to those who hurt them. Choosing love over anger was their protection against pain.

It has been my observation that folks who overcome major wounds in life often use their early woundedness to bring much beauty to their lives in later years. Many of the support groups that have evolved in the United States over the years have been founded by individuals who use their wounds to bring help and encouragement to others suffering from the same woundedness.

In his autobiography, the British writer-physician A. J. Cronin describes being a doctor in the North of England when there was an outbreak of diphtheria. A little boy was brought in hardly able to breathe. In those days that often meant the patient would die. The doctor performed a tracheotomy that allowed the child to breathe, and put him in the care of a young nurse who would watch him through the night hours. The doctor went off to bed.

In the wee hours of the morning, a trembling nurse wakened him with the sad news that the little boy was dead. Exhausting herself, the nurse had slipped into sleep only to awaken and discover that the tube was blocked and the child dead. The physician was furious. He raged against the girl. He told her he would see to it that she would never nurse again. She stood before his wrath pitifully small, devastated by what had happened, and in a pathetic voice scarcely audible said, "Give me another chance." He told her he would not, and having dismissed her, went back to bed.

Back in bed, but not to sleep. Her poor face haunted him, and so did her words, "give me another chance." And the next morning, when he got up, he tore up the letter of condemnation he had written during the night.

Years later, Cronin tells us, he met the young girl, now grown to womanhood, the matron of one of the largest children's hospitals in England and known throughout the country for her commitment to her calling and her nursing skills. It was in overcoming her woundedness that this woman created beauty in her life and in her profession.

Jewish theologian Abraham Joshua Heschel writes, "In prayer we shift the center of living from self-consciousness to self-surrender." In the beginning of a wound, sometimes it hurts so much we can't go beyond feeling it at all. But usually we find a way to tame the pain. Usually we find a way to live with, not against, the hurt.

The late Henri Nouwen wrote a short book that was very popular when I was in seminary. The title of the book is *The Wounded Healer*. The thesis of his book is that it is only out of our own hurts, sufferings, and wounds that we are able to bring compassion, empathy, wholeness, and healing to others.

In the film *The Saint of Fort Washington*, Matthew is depicted as a mentally disturbed, perhaps somewhat retarded young man who is also a wounded healer. Shunned by his family, he loses his apartment when his building is torn down. He meets Jerry, an older black man, who shows him the ropes of street survival. They discover that Matthew has healing power in his hands when he touches Jerry's arthritic knee and the pain subsides. Later, when it is raining and they find shelter with some other homeless people in an abandoned building, Jerry tells Spits, an old man with pain-wracked hands, about Matthew's power. Spits would like to give the young Puerto Rican couple, who are leaving to get married and take a job, the only present he could, a shoeshine. His calling has been shining shoes, hence his nickname. However, Spits has had to give it up because of his arthritic hands. Jerry convinces the shy, reluctant Matthew to lay his hands on Spits' hands. Matthew does, and a few minutes later Spits can feel the pain leaving him. The little group rejoices, and Jerry holds his cupped hands out a window, catching some rainwater in them. He walks over and "baptizes" the healer, calling him "St. Matthew," the saint of the streets and the homeless. Despite his slowness and mental anguish, Matthew is a healer, albeit a wounded one.

As we move into our Easter communion service this morning, I ask that we reflect upon the hurts, the sufferings, and the wounds found in each of our individual lives. Are there wounds that we have embraced and in so doing found beauty, creativity, and healing? Are there wounds that we have tried to deny or avoid? How can we more fully embrace our individual woundedness? For it is in embracing our woundedness that we often find the health, the healing, the wholeness, and the resurrection of spirit that we so earnestly seek.

16

Silence and Worship

ONE OF THE NOISIEST cities I have ever visited is Seoul, Korea. From 1984 to 1985, I endured a one-year hardship tour of duty in the Republic of Korea as an army chaplain with a mechanized infantry battalion assigned to the Second Infantry Division. I once counted the nights that I spent either sleeping in a tent or in a sleeping bag lying on the ground under the stars, and I was surprised to realize that seven months of nights of my twelve months of duty in Korea were spent sleeping in either a tent, sleeping bag on the ground, or a combination of both! If soldiers were paid overtime for all work performed beyond forty hours a week, we would all leave the army very wealthy!

Although my base was located north of Seoul near the Demilitarized Zone (DMZ), I often made visits to Seoul for meetings or to take soldiers on religious retreats. During my many visits to Seoul, I quickly learned that the custom in Korea is to use the automobile horn not to warn people that there might be an impending collision, but merely to indicate that a car is moving down the street. Especially are horns used at intersections. The driver who has the loudest and most prolonged horn tends to have the right-of-way when approaching the intersection. Not only is this noisy, but it can also be rather frightening if you happen to be the passenger in a taxi cab operated by a rather aggressive kamikaze cab driver. This is somewhat a paradox. Korea, nicknamed "the land of the morning calm," is also home to many aesthetic Buddhist temples noted for simplicity and serenity. No doubt the term "Land of the Morning Calm" was more applicable to Korea prior to the advent of Western civilization with our modern gadgets and honking automobiles.

Sampson County, North Carolina, is not Seoul, Korea, but I think you will agree that there is a lot of noise even here. Many of us have become so used to living in a world of noise that we find silence almost unbearable.

How many of you will sometimes turn on the television just to have noise in your house? How many of you dare drive to Clinton, Fayetteville, or Wilmington without turning on your car radio? And it seems that every new invention brings with it more noise—for instance, vacuum cleaners, food processors, electric can openers, and those awful stereo speakers that can be heard vibrating in your house from passing automobiles and/or hand-held so-called boom boxes.

It is not my purpose this morning to preach about noise. Perhaps there is enough noise in most preaching as it is. This morning I want to speak about that precious and blessed gift of God to us known as silence. I want us to think together about the uses of silence, and before we are finished I want us to think about the limitations of silence. The art of using silence is rapidly becoming a lost art. Yet, so important has silence been in the history of religion that we ought to hope that modern men and women can once again learn to use silence constructively.

It has been the Quakers, also known as the Friends or the Society of Friends, who seem to have learned best to use silence in a worship service. I very much like the Quakers. If I were to unite with a church other than a Universalist one, I think it would probably be either Quaker or Unity. During my two years stationed at Fort Riley, Kansas, I often visited the Quaker Society in nearby Manhattan, Kansas. I recall many services during which most of the service consisted of absolute silence. These deeply religious people take very seriously the comment of Jesus in the Gospels that "the kingdom of God is within you." The Quakers have built their service of worship around a process of introspection, a looking inward with an atmosphere of reverent silence. They believe that if one looks hard enough within sometimes the Spirit will break through the barriers between the human and the Divine, and God will speak to an individual in the silence of his or her inner being.

I have been to a couple of Quaker meetings where no one spoke for the entire hour. At the end of the hour the congregation was dismissed by a lay leader. However, as I looked upon the serenity in the faces of several in the group, it was quite apparent that some of these folks had been very close to the Heart of their Being or to that which some of us would call God.

By the way, the Quakers were not misled into thinking that everything that came from the mouth of a devout Quaker on the floor of the meeting house was a direct inspiration from God. They always assume that any revelation to an individual has to be tested by the opinion of the group. If a Quaker has something to say that he or she feels came from God, he or she utters it on the floor of the meeting, and then the meeting considers it. They do not take votes because voting is often divisive. They talk about the matter until they have a consensus of opinion. Talking about a matter until they have all agreed may seem like a lot of talking and a great waste of time when the majority could very quickly vote down the minority. But consider this fact: the Quakers through this seemingly slow process of consensus were able to free all of their slaves a hundred years before the Civil War. This was eventually a unanimous decision, and it did not involve a war. They always test the so-called speaking of God to an individual by referring it to the group so that there are no "far out" or "false prophets" who might lead them astray.

Most of us here would be scarcely able to endure an hour of concentrated silence. Most of us would find it difficult to have ten minutes of pure silence during a Sunday morning worship service. I assure you that an hour of silent worship is the longest hour you ever will spend in your life, and even if it is a productive hour, it takes great endurance if one really concentrates. I don't know if we need an hour of silence every Sunday morning, but I would be attracted to a Sunday service that allowed for extended periods of silence during the service.

Thomas Kelly, in his book *A Testament of Devotion*, suggests that there ought to be "little silences" in our lives even in the midst of the busiest schedule. There ought to be periods of composure and inward searching, even deliberate pauses for reflection and depth perception into our inner being many times during each day. It doesn't take hours of silence for silence to be effective. It takes just a moment of inward calm to set us straight and to get things back into perspective. But such short moments of silence and reflection can actually be more effective than an hour spent once a week in silence.

In an ethical sense we say that religion should not just operate one day a week and then we should live the rest of the week as we please. What Dr. Kelly is saying is that an hour on Sunday morning is a fine thing for worship, but it is more important that we use these silent periods almost every hour of every day so that we go to sleep thinking about that which we call God and we wake joyful for that which we call God. This kind of religious devotion may sound terribly pious and religious to some Unitarian Universalists, but is there any reason why mature people should not try to stretch out into more moments of their life the inspiration of their highest moments? As a Carthusian monk once wrote, "Our silence is not just emptiness and death. On the contrary, it should draw us ever nearer, to the fullness of life. We are silent because the words by which our souls would fain live cannot be expressed in earthly language."

I want to suggest first, therefore, that a primary use of silence in personal living is to get perspective on ourselves—literally to look inward and to find ourselves. Oftentimes, the person who stays abnormally busy may very well be running away from him or herself. Many people keep busy just so that they will not have to face themselves or perhaps find out who they are. If such persons spent some time probing the depths of their being in silence, they might not be so afraid of what they would find out about themselves. They might find something wonderful rather than frightening within, or if not wonderful, at least insightful. Most of what is frightening in life deals with unknowns. In silence we can look at ourselves; we can begin to put our lives into perspective; we can observe that from which we are running; and if perchance it be ourselves, we can begin to find out something about ourselves that a look in the mirror will never reveal. All of us need personal introspection, and the psychological perspective that we can get upon ourselves through the use of inner silence is important indeed.

Essentially what psychotherapy and psychoanalysis accomplish in a basic sense is a looking inward. Much of the one-year Clinical Pastoral Education residency program that I completed at Duke University Medical Center was a looking inward. One way of turning inward is to talk a great deal about the past, and this is the technique that is used a great deal by the psychoanalyst. But many of us can accomplish the same thing by taking ample time for moments of silence. We can use silence to find ourselves.

In the second place, we may discover that in our own inner being there is something that mirrors the Divine Being of the universe. In our silence we may find something beyond ourselves. It is then that silence becomes a form of prayer or meditation. The Quakers do not believe that they are acting only psychologically when they worship through silence. They find a spiritual as well as a personal meaning to silence. They believe that deep within every person there is a spark of the Divine Fire that makes every individual precious. In fact, Quakers take this belief in the divinity of every person so seriously that they use terms like "thee" and "thou," words normally reserved for God, to address each other. When one says "thee" or "thou" to another person, one is recognizing the divinity within that person.

I can think of no better way to get to God than by silent introspection, a searching quiet time when we can discover for ourselves what no one can ever tell us, that we are a spark of a Divine Fire and that not even death can quench that divine spark. Such silent introspection is a practice that we could use more often. As Dr. Kelly says, we could try "little silences" until we have learned to use them in our daily lives to give our lives perspective and meaning.

Some people are fearful that if they turn inward they will somehow become otherworldly and will turn away from reality rather than into it. This is a sad mistake, for we feel that basically the real things are what are outside ourselves in the material world. Science is almost too ready not to believe in the existence of something unless it can be weighed and measured, and yet many of the important aspects of life do not lend themselves at all to scientific treatment. For example, it is difficult to measure and weigh truth, or devotion, or love, even human love. Does that mean there is no such thing as love? To assume that the outer is real and the inner is otherworldly or an illusion is one of the great confusions of our times. I suggest, therefore, that a second use of silence is to look within to see what we may find there, and we may be surprised to discover that by turning away from the outer world, we may be turning into the reality of the inner world.

Hopefully, religion is never complete unless we go forth from here as men and women who have a new and more significant vision of the community of humanity so that we are inspired to practice our ideals in society. I mean by this that silence and turning inward is not to be an end into itself. The Quaker believes that when he or she experiences God in the simple sanctuary of his or her own inner self that this experience of God needs to be exemplified in such a way as to show other men and women that they too carry a spark of the Divine.

For most of us silence is not enough in worship. We need something more than pure silence. For many of us, there is the desire for music. Music gives us a line of tone upon which to hang the insights of silence. Read the words of our hymns. These are the words of insights of silence. Music enhances worship so that it is more meaningful to us.

As Universalists, we also like to have some intellectual and verbal content to our service of worship. This is supplied by readings and hopefully by the sermon.

But I propose that we probably need more rather than less silence in our services of worship. Sunday morning could be a training time in the discipline of silence. We ought to search more the silences of our own inner being. We ought in the words of Thomas Kelly to seek more of those precious little moments of silence in the midst of our daily lives—moments of silence which we literally create when things around us are the most hectic. It may very well be that in these moments of silence we shall find our true destiny more so than from all the words that are uttered by the minister, the policies that are adopted by denominational committees, the committee meetings that are held, and even the good deeds that we do. Let us not forget to make silence a part of our lives.

17

More Bricks, But No Straw:
Reflections on Work in the United States

THERE WERE THREE EVENTS this past week that led me to write this morning's sermon. First, a book I have been reading entitled *Work to Live*, by Joe Robinson had me already thinking about work and the lack of leisure time in America. Monday afternoon while driving to the grocery store, I listened to an NPR interview regarding new retirement hurdles for Americans. The person being interviewed was Walter Updegrave, author of *We're Not in Kansas Anymore: Strategies for Retiring Rich in a Totally Changed World*. The interview included the opportunity for listeners to call in with questions. Many of the calls were from retirees who were dealing with many of the retirement issues and hurdles to which Walter Updegrave was addressing, and I found the program quite educational. While driving back home after my grocery shopping, I listened to the news of the Senate defeat of efforts to raise the U.S. minimum wage from $5.15 an hour. (Our minimum wage has been the same since 1996.) I could not help but do the math to see what $5.15 an hour is in annual wages. By the way, if you want a simple way to figure annual wages based upon hourly wages and a forty-hour workweek, multiply the hourly wage by 2000. Thus, $5.15 an hour comes out to $10,300 in gross wages.

I could not help but compare this minimal annual wage to what I now have to pay for the government-subsidized COBRA health insurance for Nataliya and me which is $8,000 a year. This plan is only good for eighteen months, but I took this coverage because it is the only insurance I could find that would cover preexisting conditions and cover Nataliya since she has less than twelve full months of residency in the United States. The cost for this plan is the same whether you are a private or a general. So what if I am a young private first class or buck sergeant coming off active duty with a family, and the only work I can find is minimum wage? Do you think I can spend $8,000 of my annual $10,300 gross wages for health insurance?

In doing research for this morning's sermon, I found that comparable nonsubsidized family health insurance coverage plans average about $12,485 a year. So, if you divide $12,485 by 2000 you find that a sole family bread earner or a single parent needs at least $6.25 per hour in take-home pay just to pay for family health insurance. So, I guess if you don't eat; don't need any clothes because you live in a nudist colony; if you can walk to work (and I guess you will have to work at the nudist colony since you don't have any clothes), and if you can live in a tent for free at the nudist colony, I assume you and your family might be able to make ends meet on $12,485 a year until you and your family eventually die of starvation since you have no money for food. But, you have to be making $1.10 more in take-home wages than the minimum wage for even this plan to work!

As an aside, when I shared the first draft of today's sermon with several friends via the Internet, a friend from Florida wrote me back and shared with me the research provided by Barbara Ehrenreich, a journalist who went "underground" in a series of minimum-wage jobs around the country: a waitress, a maid in a franchised maid business, and a Wal-Mart employee. The title of her book that details her undercover work is *Nickel and Dimed*. She details how it is impossible to get by. She includes what people go through just for a place to live while they're working these jobs. For example, many people working in the fast food restaurant business are actually living out of their cars or sharing fleabag motel rooms with virtual strangers from other shifts just to have a roof over their heads.

In writing today's sermon, I decided to go with the energy I was feeling around my reading of Joe Robinson's book, the retirement issues interview on NPR, the news of the defeat of an increase in minimum wage, and my personal frustrations with the U.S. health care system. I've entitled this sermon "More Bricks, But No Straw: Reflections on Work in the United States."

The reference to more bricks, but no straw does not refer to the children's story about the three little pigs, the big bad wolf, and the houses made of straw and brick, although with some creativity perhaps I could have used this children's story as a text for this morning's sermon. Actually, the title relates to the Exodus account of the Hebrew people under bondage in ancient Egypt. Allow me to read from the Old Testament book of Exodus, chapter 5, verses 1–9.

> Moses and Aaron went to the king of Egypt and told him, "The LORD God says, 'Let my people go into the desert, so they can honor me with a celebration there.'" Who is this LORD and why should I obey him?" the king replied. "I refuse to let you and your people go!"
>
> They answered, "The LORD God of the Hebrews has appeared to us. Please let us walk three days into the desert where we can offer sacrifices to him. If you don't, he may strike us down with terrible troubles or with war."
>
> The king said, "Moses and Aaron, why are you keeping these people from working? Look how many you are keeping from doing their work. Now everyone get back to work!"
>
> That same day the king gave orders to his slave bosses and to the men directly in charge of the Israelite slaves. He told them:
>
> "Don't give the slaves any more straw to put in their bricks. Force them to find their own straw wherever they can, but they must make the same number of bricks as before. They are lazy, or else they would not beg me to let them go and sacrifice to their God. Make them work so hard that they won't have time to listen to these lies." (Exod 5:1–9)

I want to suggest to you this morning that the average worker in the United States today shares much in common with the frustrations of the early Hebrew people in ancient Egypt when the Pharaoh ordered the same production of bricks but without the straw necessary for brick production. Before I go any further this morning, I want you to recall a time in your life when you were in a work situation and you felt overstressed, overworked, and trapped. You disliked your job but at the same time were afraid of losing your job, and you felt little hope for the future. Think about a time when you would wake up in the middle of the night and have difficulty getting back to sleep because of worrying about job-related issues and/or personal financial issues. Are you able to visualize that time in your life? Unfortunately, for some of you that unpleasant time is now. For others of you who are retired, that difficult time was years ago. However, whenever this difficult time you recall was for you, please know that for a majority of American workers in 2005 this difficult time is now.

For many American workers, despite dual-income families, the American dream has turned into a nightmare of work without end, where sixty-two percent of U.S. workers reports being stressed from work overload. We are seeing the buying power of our wages diminishing. Health care costs are rising faster than the rate of inflation, yet many American workers are finding their employment-based health insurance coverage reduced, with employees facing higher premiums and higher deductibles, while an increasing number of employers are opting to provide no health insurance for their employees. Fewer companies are providing pension funds for their employees, and the age of receiving full social security benefits is slated to increase for baby boomers and those who will follow the boomers. Many retired American workers who thought they had a safe and secure retirement with a company pension are finding that their pensions are one of the first things to go when their ex-employer files for bankruptcy. And even sick leave and vacation leave are benefits that are becoming increasingly rare in the American work force.

We have adult workers going to work sick because they have no sick leave. We have children going to school sick because their parents have no family leave enabling them to stay home with a sick child.

Indeed, there are many working parents in the United States today who have no means of taking paid leave to care for a sick child. There are many working parents in the United States today who have no means of taking paid leave when they are too sick to come in to work, so they either come to work sick, stay home without pay, or in some cases stay home without pay and risk being fired.

The stress American workers feel today has a tremendous negative impact upon what religious folks call spirituality. American workers have less and less time for honoring and nurturing our relationships with significant others, family members, and friends. We have less time and energy for volunteer civic organizations and parent teacher associations. We have less time for religious activities. We don't have time for going to church on Sunday mornings because for many American workers, Sunday has become the only day of the week for washing clothes, paying bills, cleaning the house, and grocery shopping. Most importantly, we have less time for doing what the Psalmist describes as "being still and knowing God." Our lives have become out of balance, and this means our sense of the spiritual dimension in life is no longer an aspect of our daily awareness.

Allow me to share with you some alarming statistics:

1. In 2005, almost half the American work force doesn't have paid sick days.

2. The United States spends at least 40 percent more per capita on health care than any other industrialized country in the world, yet the United States ranks poorly relative to other industrialized nations in health care despite having the best-trained health care providers and the best medical infrastructure of any industrialized nation. A recent ranking in the *Economist* magazine listed the United States in twenty-third place among all nations of the world in terms of overall health care, compared to France with first place. Eighty-eight percent of the U.S. population expresses dissatisfaction with their experiences in trying to access and utilize health care in the United States.

3. Forty percent of the American work force is now working more than 50 hours a week. In fact, we are now working more hours a year than Americans have worked since 1920. Projections call for us to be working 60 hours a week by 2010.

4. American workers were working 163 more hours a year in the early 1990s than in 1967. The number jumped to 182 more hours by the end of the 1990s.

5. Approximately 45 million Americans, or 15.6 percent of the population, were without health insurance coverage during the entire year of 2003.

6. Health insurance premiums are rising at their highest rate of increase since 1991. Recent increases in health insurance premiums are associated with decreases in health coverage.

7. The ratio of CEO-to-worker pay quadrupled from 1980 to 2000, from 42 times median worker pay to a boggling 500 times. Thus, for the median male American's income of $39,792 in 2000 ($40,668 in 2003), the typical American CEO was paid an annual pay package of $19,896,000. This week's *Economist* magazine has a cover story stating that the bonuses paid our nation's top 100 CEOs increased by over 46 percent this past year, for an average increase of over 1.14 million dollars. Thus, the typical American CEO's pay package is now over 21 million dollars a year.

8. The United States has the most unequal distribution of income and wealth, and the fastest growing gap between the rich and the poor, in all developed countries.

9. The United States is the only country in the industrialized world without a minimum-paid-leave law.

10. While Europeans and Australians enjoy a minimum of four weeks of annual vacation time each year, American vacation leave averages only 8.1 days per year after one year on the job and only 10.2 days per year after three years on the job. Twenty-six percent of all American workers take no annual vacation time.

11. Americans now work eight to twelve more weeks a year in total hours than do our European peers.

12. Since the 1970s, the typical dual-income family has increased its annual total of working hours by 684 hours, or the equivalent of four months of full-time work.

13. In 2004, 43 percent of American families spent more than they earned.

14. Household liability as a percentage of disposable income is at its highest level ever in the United States. On average, Americans spend $1.22 for every dollar they earn.

Enough depressing statistics for now! In fact, those are enough depressing statistics to last a lifetime! And my younger brother Joseph, who is a paramedic, warned me that these statistics alone might be so distressing to hear that some in the congregation might find their lifetimes ending this morning. When I sent Joseph a draft of this sermon, he asked me not to preach it. He said Americans don't want to hear how bad things really are. But before this sermon is over, I *hope* to give you *hope* that the future for American workers doesn't have to be as bad as the present.

I've really appreciated the opportunity to spend some extended time in Europe these past four years. For me, nothing compares to the experience of living in a foreign country to gain insight and new perspectives concerning life and living in one's own country. I wish all our young men and women were given the opportunity to spend at least one year living, working, studying, and traveling in a foreign land. However, I want to clarify my wish by stating that wearing a uniform and living in Iraq for a year is not what I had in mind as the way for our young men and women to have the enriching experience of living overseas.

In all seriousness, my heart goes out to our young men and women in uniform who are serving in Iraq and Afghanistan this morning, forty percent of whom are Army Reserve and National Guard soldiers who never dreamed they would be mobilized for fifteen months and spend twelve months separated from family and friends while deployed in a war zone. My heart goes out to the family members of our young men and women in uniform who are in Iraq and Afghanistan this morning. The challenges faced by family members are equally difficult. I know. For sixteen months I recently worked with the spouses and children of active-duty deployed soldiers who had been based in Germany prior to their deployments. What a challenge some of these young couples and young families are facing!

To mention our young men and women in uniform and their family members this morning is not necessarily digressing from this morning's sermon topic. Oftentimes when I have talked with a young active-duty soldier or the young spouse of a deployed active-duty soldier, the questions, why did you join the Army? or, why did you and your spouse join the Army? often come up in conversations. I'd say that in ninety percent of the occasions the responses to these questions related to their difficulties in finding a good job with health care benefits back in these United States. For many of America's young, joining the military, even if it means the likelihood of going to war, is seen as the only solution to the problem of finding a livable wage that includes health care benefits and money for college. I know the Army needs recruits. The Army desperately needs new recruits. Thus far for this year, the active Army, the Army Reserve, and the National Guard are all falling short of their recruiting goals. But I think it is a national shame when the primary reason a young man or woman feels compelled to join the military is because he or she can't find a decent job with health care benefits in these United States.

Well, let's go back to life in Europe. Most Europeans have an entirely different concept of work than we have in the United States. Europeans work to live. They don't live to work.

I want you to imagine this morning any American social setting in which strangers are meeting for the first time. Question number one for most Americans is, what's your name? Well, question number one is the same for Americans and Europeans, but it is question number two that is strikingly different between American and European strangers meeting for the first time. For Americans, question number two is, what do you do? or, where do you work? However, if you ask question number two as the second question in a European setting, it doesn't go over as well. In fact, it would be quite a shock and even impolite to rush into the issue of employment that immediately. Europeans identify themselves more in terms of their private life—family, where they're from, social activities, and hobbies—than they do their jobs.

I got to know several native Germans through my ministry to the English-speaking Unitarian Universalist Congregation in Heidelberg. Nataliya and I were invited and we attended several parties and dinners in the homes of members of the congregation in which several Germans were in attendance. In fact, in many of the couples in the congregation one spouse was a German national. At German social gatherings the topic of work is rarely discussed. What is discussed is family, the next Volksmarch, hot air ballooning, the last vacation, and plans for the next vacation. At first, I found these conversations awkward, partly because I am accustomed to talking more about work in social settings, but I also came to realize, like most Americans, that I did not have much of a life outside of the life I knew as work. This was a difficult personal revelation for me to accept.

Earlier I shared with you the statistic that forty percent of the American work force is now working more than fifty hours a week. Guess what? In the countries comprising the European Union it is illegal to work more than forty-eight hours a week. Workaholism is considered stupid, not only because it's a threat to personal health and family, but also because it's counterproductive to quality performance in the work-place. The belief is that workaholics drive, not profits, but the stress of everyone around them, which causes frayed interpersonal relations and reduced productivity. One firm in Belgium has a program that identifies and roots out workaholics and then guides them through a course in simmering down. What a contrast to American culture where we tend to glorify workaholism. Why do we Americans tend to prize ourselves as workaholics?

In his book *Work to Live*, author Joe Robinson points to studies that have shown for over eighty years that long hours and unrested workers provide diminishing returns.

There are hundreds of studies that have shown that human beings are no longer productive and cost effective to their employers when working more than forty-eight hours a week. Also, once you go beyond forty-eight hours a week for an extended period of time, most human beings begin to experience health problems that cost both the employer and the employee more money. This brings us to the subject of health care.

I don't have time this morning to fully embrace the health care issue, but let me simply add that Europeans do not have the worries over health care and health care insurance that American have. Every citizen of a nation comprising the European Union is covered with health insurance, either a government plan or a private plan, and their health plans cover more of the medical expenses than do our American plans. And guess what? Their costs for health care are nearly half what it is for Americans. Two reasons for this are that (1) in the United States the insured pay for the costs of medical care for the uninsured, and (2) private for-profit insurance companies in the United States are greedy, with top insurance executives making tremendously huge salaries. Private for-profit insurance companies in the United States spend twenty to thirty percent of what we pay in premiums on administration and profits to include the big salaries that are paid for those at the top. This compares to the three percent the U.S. government pays to handle Medicare administration costs. All of the administrative costs to include the salaries of the government employees who work with Medicare only cost three percent of the Medicare budget. Many of us complain about the waste in our government bureaucracies, but the waste in government spending doesn't come close to the financial leeching Americans receive at the hands of private for-profit insurance companies and managed health care companies. More bricks, but no straw! Well, we could do a series of sermons regarding health care in the United States, but we will leave it at that for now. Let's go back to Europe.

Another difference between Americans and Europeans (and in fact I think it is actually a difference between Americans and the rest of the world) is that Americans tend to be more inclined to live for the future. We tend to believe that it's all going to happen tomorrow. If we just work harder and longer and give up more nights and weekends and bang our heads just a little more we'll get that promotion, money, status, house, and/or car of our dreams, and then we'll be "there," where the struggle and sacrifice will have been worth it. Americans tend to live for a future that never quite arrives, and in the meantime, life goes on without us. We lose touch with friends and have no time to make new ones. Relationships and children are sacrificed for careers. Passions and hobbies are lost in the rat race. We miss out on scores of experiences to learn and explore and keep life new. We forget what fun is. The months turn into years of postponement.

In my twenty-nine years of ministry, I've seen this happen far too often. Folks die while waiting for this future time when they think they will finally live. I have buried many a parishioner in his or her fifties or early sixties who died before reaching that future time when they were planning to finally live.

Among Europeans, as well as what I've seen with people in every other place I've visited on this planet, there is the tendency to live more in the here and now. Evenings and weekends are times to play and have fun. In Europe, department stores and grocery stores are closed on Sunday, and until very recently, they were closed on Saturday afternoons. So different from the United States where we have become accustomed to 24/7 shopping.

In Germany, every little town has some festival every few months. The festival will begin on Thursday evening and conclude on Sunday and will include music, dancing, food, local beer and wine, and the selling of local crafts. And even with the open sale of beer and wine, I rarely saw anyone intoxicated, and the few times I did, the drunken person was usually an American who was attending the event.

Nataliya and I had an apartment in the Heidelberg suburb of Leimen. Many evenings we would walk into the mountains overlooking Leimen and Heidelberg. In fact, on a clear day you could see across the Rhine River into France. The Germans have elaborate hiking trails all through their mountains. As we walked we would encounter entire German families out walking for evening recreation as well as younger Germans on trail bikes pedaling up and coasting down the mountain slopes. On many a spring and fall day, we could count four or five hot air balloons in the late afternoon sky.

I recall one late-February Saturday morning in 2004. I was returning to our apartment after running at a local sports track. In the distance, I heard the sound of something resembling a marching band or maybe a mixture of marching band and carnival type music. As I came closer, I encountered a parade with adults and children in all sorts of different costumes, many carrying balloons, walking down the street. Several of the parade participants were throwing pieces of candy to those who stood on the sidewalk. At first, I thought the parade might be related to Mardi Gras, but I quickly realized that Mardi Gras was already past. About midway in the parade, I recognized an American family who were members of the Heidelberg Unitarian Universalist congregation, and I called to them. Ruth Ann, the mother, walked out of the parade and came over to where I was standing.

"What is this parade about?" I asked her.

Ruth Ann responded. "Oh, this is just something Leimen has every February to celebrate that winter is almost over. Isn't it great?"

Then she excused herself and rejoined her husband and two children as they progressed down the street. Here were a hundred or so folks in the parade and another several hundred folks standing on the sidewalks taking time for a Saturday morning parade just to celebrate that winter was almost over! So very un-American! For most Americans there are more work-related things to do than join a Saturday-morning parade to celebrate that winter is almost over.

Earlier I alluded to the fact that the United States has no minimum-paid-leave law, which means that no U.S. employer is required by law to give any worker paid vacation or sick leave. Well, let's compare that standard with the rest of the world. In communist China the law mandates fifteen days of vacation a year, and the average Chinese worker takes fifteen days of vacation. In Japan the law mandates ten days of vacation, and the average Japanese worker takes seventeen and a half days. In Spain the law mandates twenty-five days of vacation a year, and the average Spanish worker takes thirty. In the United Kingdom the law mandates twenty days of vacation a year, and the average British worker takes twenty-five. In Italy the law mandates twenty days of vacation a year, and the average Italian worker takes thirty. And in France, bless their hearts, the law mandates twenty-five days of vacation a year, and the average French worker takes between thirty-two and forty-two days of vacation. This compares to the average American worker who has been with the same employer for at least three years taking only 10.2 days of vacation per year and the sad fact that twenty-six percent of all Americans take no vacation at all.

Among career army officers and senior noncommissioned officers, there has become an annual August and September ritual known as "burning leave." You see, there is a limited amount of leave that an active-duty soldier can carry from one fiscal year to the next fiscal year. This policy was enacted to encourage soldiers to take vacation. However, the workaholic ethic among senior career soldiers has twisted this policy. When a career-minded officer or noncommissioned officer finds him or herself in the situation of having to use or lose annual leave in August and September, he or she will announce to his or her peers and especially to his or her superiors that he or she will be burning leave. It is an important part of this ritual that you announce to others what you are doing before you do it. Now, guess what the soldier does while "burning" this excess leave? He or she gets a leave slip signed for the number of days of leave that must be used and then he or she commences to continue coming to work during the leave period. Of course, it is appropriate when burning leave to arrive at work an hour or so later in the morning and it is appropriate to leave an hour or so earlier in the evening. Also, it is OK to come to work wearing your physical training (PT) uniform instead of the standard battle dress uniform. While burning leave you put in an eight-to-ten-hour day of work instead of the usual twelve-to-fourteen -hour day. On the military base where I worked in Germany, there were two buildings that housed the offices of the NATO contingent in Heidelberg. There were a few officers and noncommissioned officers from all the NATO countries present at our base. Now, I can't begin to tell you how much puzzlement and amusement this ritual of burning leave brings to our British, Canadian, Dutch, German, Italian, Norwegian, Spanish, and especially our French NATO allied soldiers. They think of it as being absolutely crazy, and it is crazy.

My friends, we have become a nation of workaholics who spend more money than we earn, and we have come to neglect those activities in life that bring joy and love and meaning and spiritual awareness to our lives. If our bodies and souls were automobiles, it would be appropriate to say that we are running on empty.

So why do we do it? Why do we spend our entire lifetimes working? Maybe we don't know any better. Since only twenty percent of Americans even own passports, an even fewer number of Americans have actually traveled abroad to see and experience this difference in mindset regarding work. I confess: Five years ago I prided myself on the fact that I was able to work a forty-hour-a-week job as a prison chaplain, work another twenty hours a week as a part-time parish minister, and work another one weekend a month and two to four weeks a year as a U.S. Army Reserve Chaplain. I averaged over seventy hours a week of work, and I rarely took a day off. I'd often volunteer to work at the prison on holidays because I could get time-and-a-half pay for holiday work.

Over the three-year period preceding 2001, guess how many concerts and movies I attended? Guess how many novels I read just for fun? Guess how many birthday parties I attended for nephews and nieces? Guess how many videos I checked out from Blockbuster to watch on weekends? Guess how many television shows I watched at night? The answer is zero. Why is the answer zero? Because I thought work was more important. During this three-year period the only reading I did was to keep up on current events and to do research for sermon writing and stock market investing. The only television I watched was morning news. I remember attending a church conference in 2000, and one of the small group ice-breaker questions was to share with the group your favorite hobby. I was surprised to realize that I no longer had any hobbies outside work. I've come to realize that extreme work hours and skipping vacations prove only one thing: you don't value yourself.

In his book *Work to Live*, Joe Robinson writes, "busyness is the nation's real business. It has become a goal in and of itself. Workaholism, chronic busyness, and productivity mania fools us into believing that we are making the most of our time with all the action, when in truth we're actually squandering life."

In our busyness and workaholism, we are missing out on the very essence of life: nurturing our soul, nurturing those relationships with the people we love, having fun, being creative, and taking time to be still and know God.

So, I will conclude my sermon with words of hope.

1. American workaholism is not the norm in the rest of the world. In most of the rest of the world, people work to live. They don't live to work. When we read the Genesis story of creation, whether you believe the story or not, there is value in the story. God Almighty, the Creator of the Universe, Ultimate Being, our Higher Power, or the Mystery of the Universe—whatever term you prefer to refer to God—according to Genesis took a day off to rest after creating the world. If God—be God Yahweh or Allah—requires a twenty-four-hour time of rest after working the previous week, don't you think we mortals need the same? We Americans need to reject the 24/7 work mentality. It is stupid and it is killing us. I encourage each one of you to begin thinking creatively as to how *you* can change your mindset from living to work to working to live. Begin this next week with a commitment to take one twenty-four-hour period when you do not work or think about work. Use this twenty-four-

hour period to rest, to rediscover your soul, to renew your spirit, to nurture those special relationships in your life, and to reclaim those activities or hobbies that can bring creativity, joy, and fun back into your life.

2. My second word of hope deals with personal debt. Americans are the biggest consumers on the planet. If the rest of the world can live and have a balanced life without buying so much *stuff* on credit, so can you and I. Stop using credit cards to buy stuff you don't really need. The truth is that the more we own, the more our possessions own us. Do we really need that new car? Do we really need that larger house? The more in debt you are, the more you feel enslaved to work more. One surprise that greeted me when I returned to the United States this past year was the price of groceries. You can now buy a grocery cart full of Chinese-made electronic gadgets for less money than you can buy a grocery cart full of groceries. Consider planting a garden this spring. Not only will a garden save you thousands of dollars in grocery bills, but also tending to a garden can be a wonderful means for reigniting your spiritual life. There is something we gain that is both mystical and divine when we involve ourselves in the mystery of life as we witness seeds sprout into plants and plants into blossoms and blossoms into vegetables and fruit. Plus, the vegetables and fruits we grow from our own garden will be a lot healthier than what we buy at the grocery store. Tending a garden can be a family activity that helps build family bonds.

3. My third word of hope is that we must lobby our government. Our congressmen and senators listen when Democrat, Republican, and Independent voters come together on an issue. Having a health care system that works and having paid family and sick leave are not Democratic issues or Republican issues. These are American issues. These issues represent family values as well as worker concerns. Write your representatives in the Congress and the Senate and tell them you want our health care system fixed. Tell them you want a law passed that will mandate that American workers be provided a few paid days each year for family and personal sickness. Also, American workers must have livable wages. If a corporation can afford to pay its CEO 21 million dollars a year, this same corporation should be able to pay all of its employees livable wages. If a corporation can't afford to pay all its employees livable wages, then the corporation's CEO and other top executives should have their pay packages cut so that the employees can have livable wages.

4. And my fourth word of hope dovetails with my previous suggestion: I encourage you to join and support organizations that are already working to remedy these problems in our work force and with our health care system. The more members these organizations have, the more influence they have in presenting their arguments in Washington.

In the Exodus story, the Hebrew people eventually refused to continue making bricks without straw. With God's help, the Hebrew people rose up and they allowed Moses to lead them out of Egypt and into the Promised Land. America is a great country with great people and great resources, but we can't continue making more bricks without straw. It's killing us both physically and spiritually.

Change the way you think about work. Begin working to live and stop living to work. Make yourself take time off each week for rest and spiritual renewal. Don't increase your debt, and try to begin getting out of debt. And do what you can to influence our government to bring much-needed reforms to our workforce laws and our very expensive, but very dysfunctional health care system.

Reform can and will come, but change will only come when Americans, as individuals and as a society, change our view of work and come together with one voice and proclaim, "No more bricks without straw!"

Delivered on March 13, 2005, at Clayton Memorial Unitarian Universalist Church, Newberry, South Carolina.

18

Universalism and Purgatory

W HEN YOU COME TO think about it, Universalism has its beginnings around the issue of death. Universalism is an answer to the question, what happens to the soul at death? Is there a hell? Is there a heaven? Is there a soul that transcends the experience of human death? If there is such a soul, what happens to this soul following the death of the human body? These are questions that often nag at us from just beneath our conscious thought. However, when confronted with death—be it the death of a loved one or our own deaths—these questions have a way of resurfacing in our consciousness. The Universalist answers to these questions are (1) yes, there is a human soul that transcends the death of the human body; and (2) there is no scriptural basis or rational basis for a belief in an eternal hell for our souls following the event of human death. However, different Universalists have held slightly different views as to just what does happen to the soul following human death.

(To the reader: the next three pages are quite similar to the early history of Universalism you read in the sermon "What Is Universalism." If you prefer, please skip the next three pages and begin reading again at the section alluding to the early Universalists who believed in "limited punishment" or purgatory in the afterlife.)

First, I'd like for us to briefly review the early history of Universalism. In early Christianity, there were various Christian groups that embraced aspects of a "Universalist" philosophy. The early Christian theologians Clement of Alexandria and Origen both embraced the doctrine of universal salvation. It was not until AD 544 that Universalism was officially labeled a heresy by the Catholic Church.

From AD 544 until the time of the Reformation, there continued to be individuals who embraced a Universalist philosophy but who were discreet in how they expressed these beliefs. After all, even those who believed in universal salvation did not cherish the idea of being burned at the stake for heresy. In the 1700s it was among the Methodists in England that the heresy of Universalism occasionally found expression. And when an English Methodist minister was found to be preaching Universalism, his preaching credentials were quickly withdrawn. And here we find the beginnings of the Universalist Church as an organized religious denomination. There was a James Relly, who had been converted to Methodism by the Methodist evangelist George Whitfield. Relly worked with Whitfield for a number of years until he and Whitfield disagreed over the issue of universal salvation. Relly left the Methodist church but continued his own brand of universalism until his death in 1778 at the age of fifty-six. He also wrote a book entitled *Union*. Remember this book *Union*; you will hear about it again.

Now there was another Englishman, John Murray, born in 1741, reared in the Calvinist religion, who as a young man attained a license to preach in the Methodist Church. As a young Methodist preacher, Murray hated those who embraced Universalism. However, after coming across and reading a copy of Relly's book *Union*, Murray began to have some ambivalent feelings about his orthodox faith. In 1757, Murray attended his first service led by James Relly, and by 1760 he had become a complete convert to what was then known as Rellyism. Of course, he was shortly thereafter voted out of his Methodist society.

After being asked to leave the Methodist Church, several other tragedies came to bear on John Murray. Although history does not record the details, Murray was arrested for debt, which he somehow managed to pay after his arrest. Then followed the death of his only son at the age of one. His wife's health began to decline and she later died. Within this same five-year period, Murray was to lose a brother and three sisters. Depression and loneliness plagued Murray. He often thought of suicide. It was only his relationship with James Relly that seemed to sustain him. Relly continually urged Murray to be a spokesman for universalism, but Murray no longer had any interest in preaching. He heard stories about the new world of America. He yearned to leave England and all his sad memories and live out the remainder of his years in obscurity in the wilderness of America.

John Murray's decision to come to America was an essentially negative one—to avoid further misery rather than to seek happiness. On a Saturday evening, July 21, 1770, he sailed from England on board the brig *Hand-in-Hand*, with a little money, some clothes, a Bible, a bundle of his late wife's letters, and various other papers.

On the other side of the Atlantic was a colorful character, considered a little crazy by his neighbors, by the name of Thomas Potter. Potter was not an educated man, but he was deeply religious, with an attraction to mysticism. Potter had made a small fortune from the lumber business and had used some of his earnings to build a meeting house for itinerant or traveling preachers to use. He had been reared as a Baptist, but had somehow come across a copy of Relly's book *Union*. In building his meeting house, Potter genuinely believed that God would eventually send him a preacher who preached universalism.

Murray's ship was to have sailed to New York, but by mistake the captain sailed to Philadelphia. From Philadelphia the ship set sail for New York, but it became grounded on a sandbar off Cranberry Inlet in Barnegat Bay on the southern coast of New Jersey. This just happened to be where Thomas Potter lived and where he had built his meeting house. While the ship was grounded, Murray went ashore with others to seek provisions. Murray met Potter, and there was sufficient conversation for Potter to learn that Murray embraced a Universalist theology. Potter begged Murray to preach. Murray refused. Murray said that he intended to leave for New York just as soon as the wind changed allowing the ship to sail from the sandbar. Finally Potter told Murray, "The wind will never change, sir, until you have delivered to us, in that meeting house, a message from God." Three days later the wind had still not changed, and Murray consented to preach in Potter's meeting house. And he continued preaching. In 1779 he formed the first Universalist Church.

Murray's church was the first organized Universalist church in America, but Universalism as an idea had been popping up a lot in America. Some who advocated it then later became a part of this new denomination. One such preacher was Elhanan Winchester, a Baptist preacher whose first pastorate was near the Great Pee Dee River in South Carolina, just a few miles from Bennettsville. There he shocked his parish and shortened his tenure by teaching the slaves and even inviting them to church. Winchester moved to Philadelphia, where he met another preacher/physician who had been preaching a mystical universalism for several years in Pennsylvania. This man's name was George de Benneville.

De Benneville embraced a mystical Universalist theology following an incident years earlier when he had been mistakenly taken for dead when in fact he was in a deep coma. It was after he had been placed in his coffin that de Benneville awoke from his coma and startled his mourners by climbing out of the coffin. De Benneville had vivid memories of his three days in the coma, and for him this near-death experience was a religious revelation. What he later wrote describing this unusual experience is quite similar to the out-of-body experiences collected by Elizabeth Kubler-Ross in recent times. At any rate, all three of these men, Murray, Winchester, and de Benneville eventually met and became spokesmen for the newly formed Universalist Church in America.

Now, I want to stop here and get back to this morning's sermon topic. All of the above-mentioned early Universalists—from Clement of Alexandria and Origen to James Relly, John Murray, Thomas Potter, Elhanan Winchester, and George de Benneville—all expressed a belief in Universalism that included a belief in what was often called "limited punishment" for the soul following human death. These early Universalists believed that, eventually, all souls would be reunited with that which we call God, but they also believed that most souls would require some limited punishment prior to that reunion with God. In fact, George de Benneville based his belief concerning limited punishment on what he saw during that near-death experience when he believed his soul left his body and a spirit guide took him on a journey into the afterlife. He claims that he witnessed souls undergoing anguish and suffering as a result of their earthly sins, but his spirit guide instructed him that the anguish and suffering these souls were experiencing were remedial in nature and that eventually these troubled souls would find reunion with God.

It was not until the time of Hosea Ballou that some Universalists rejected the idea of limited punishment for the soul following human death. Hosea Ballou preached what was known as "ultra-Universalism." He preached that there was no need for punishment in the afterlife because sin brings its own misery in this life. However, neither John Murray nor Elhanan Winchester nor George de Benneville ever adopted Ballou's ultra-Universalism position. Murray, Winchester, and de Benneville continued to preach of a limited punishment for souls following human death.

Now another term for this limited punishment is the Catholic term *purgatory*. What is purgatory? According to Catholic teaching, purgatory simply means "purging" and refers to the final purging of sin and self-love before we are face to face with God. According to the *Catholic Encyclopedia*, neither the nature nor the duration of purgatory is specified in Catholic doctrine.

According to Dr. Ken Vincent, a retired professor of psychology and a frequent writer for the *Universalist Herald*, the theology of virtually all ancient and contemporary religions includes some form of judgment for souls following the death experience. My research has found much in common with Dr. Vincent's investigations regarding the dark sides of spiritually transformative experiences and near-death experiences.

A friend of mine shared the book *The Holy Souls* with me, and I found the book fascinating. In fact, I went out and bought ten copies so I could get a fifteen-percent discount, and I loaned copies out to several folks thinking that they would find the book as fascinating as I did. To my surprise, some of you did not find the book nearly as fascinating as I did. Now, I will confess that the book is written in heavy Catholic theological language and I tended to overlook some of the entries in the book. But overall the book forced me to reconsider my beliefs about limited punishment or purgatory. During the past two weeks, I have been doing some research on this idea of purgatory. I have been amazed to learn that the concept of purgatory goes by different names in almost all religious traditions except for Protestant Christianity and Ultra-Universalism.

Both Jews and Muslims refer to purgatory as "the grave." Jews and Muslims believe that "the grave" is a time of suffering during which the soul experiences discomfort, pain, and agony for unresolved sins. Hinduism includes a belief in a place between the first death and the second death. At the second death, the soul returns to the Godhead to be reincarnated. However, between the first and second death, the soul must deal with the sins and negative karma of the earthly life. Buddhists hold a similar view of the afterlife. Within Native American religions, there is the belief in the other side. Native Americans teach that when a person dies the soul initially goes to the other side where it must first spend a period of time recalling and learning from the mistakes of one's earthly life before the soul returns to the Great White Spirit. And within metaphysical teachings is the idea of the astral world. The astral world is a place where a soul slowly becomes accustomed to the afterlife. It is a place and time for the soul to cast off its past earthly memory patterns, behaviors, and desires. According to metaphysical teachings, it is in the astral world that the soul will judge and examine every experience, moment, and instance of its recently departed life. For some souls who lived their earthly lives governed by injustice, cruelty, and hate, the astral world can take on some hellish characteristics, or so it is reported by some metaphysicians.

Let me briefly tell you about the book *The Holy Souls*. The book portrays the life and ministry of Padre Pio, who was born in 1887 in the province of Benevento in Italy and began his studies to become a Catholic priest in 1903. Padre Pio was ordained to the priesthood in 1910. He died in 1968. His entire ministry was spent in Italy, and his ministry was a controversial one. The controversy was twofold. From his early days as a priest until his death, Padre Pio claimed to have a gift for seeing and communicating with the apparitions of souls in purgatory. The book *The Holy Souls* tells of many of his encounters and conversations with these souls and what he learned regarding purgatory from his visits from these various souls. The second controversy surrounding Padre Pio was that as his ability to see apparitions strengthened, his body developed what is known as stigmata. Wounds appeared on his hands that might resemble wounds made by a nail that had been hammered through his hands. Having stigmata is rare in the Catholic religion, but it sometimes will happen to an individual who very closely identifies with the crucified Jesus. Modern medical science might call it a psychosomatic illness, but it appears that this affliction does occasionally occur with great rarity among very ardent and devout Catholic believers.

Call me naive and gullible, but after reading this book, I was left with the conviction that this man actually experienced that which he claims. His interpretation of these supernatural events are heavily clothed in Catholic language and theology, and considering the heat that the Catholic Church was giving him over these claims, it does not surprise me that he probably went to great lengths to try and interpret these experiences in a language that was compatible with Catholic doctrine. And the Catholic hierarchy did give Padre Pio a very difficult time during most of the years of his ministry. For a number of years the Catholic hierarchy forbade Padre Pio from celebrating Mass in the presence of the public, and they later forbade him from answering any personal letters that were mailed to him. It was only during the last ten years of his life that many in the Catholic hierarchy came to recognize that Padre Pio was not mentally ill and that his experiences with souls in purgatory might be real phenomenon. Today Padre Pio is revered within the Catholic Church, and there are several Padre Pio centers that have been established across the world to honor his work and his unique ministry.

There were two primary ideas expressed in this book. One idea, which is the subject of this sermon, is the reality of purgatory. The second idea that Padre Pio taught is the importance of praying for deceased loved ones. After doing some research, I have found the teaching to pray for our deceased loved ones to be a universal teaching in other religious traditions outside Protestant Christianity. Even within Protestant Christianity, there are a few denominations that teach the importance of praying for the dead. These include the Anglicans, Episcopalians, Lutherans, and the Mormons. I will share with you that since reading this teaching from Padre Pio, I have begun including short prayers for deceased loves ones in my morning devotional routine. I will light one or more votive candles for the person or persons for whom I am praying and devote some of my devotional time for reflecting upon the lives of these deceased loved ones. What are a few minutes of my time in the morning to pray for deceased loved ones if there is a possibility that their souls need my prayers? And even if there is nothing to this teaching, I have found that the time I spend reflecting upon the lives of deceased loved ones has helped keep the specialness and memories of these persons alive in my thoughts.

Well, back to the concept of purgatory: if there is a purgatory or a limited punishment for souls after this human life, how does that impact our earthly life?

One teaching of Padre Pio to which I think all Universalists can agree is that human life is a very precious experience. To be alive is a very wonderful gift. Each moment is precious. Once we are dead, we are dead. We should live each day to the fullest, and we should live each day with the awareness that our mortal life is temporary. What matters is our spiritual life. How loving are we as human beings? Do we respond to the needs of others in a loving manner? Are we holding on to past resentments? Who are the individuals with whom we have unresolved differences? Who are the individuals from whom we need forgiveness? Who are the individuals whom we need to forgive? In the words of Padre Pio, "Let us do penance in this life, so that it may not be necessary in the next."

Once Padre Pio was asked, "Padre, how can I suffer Purgatory here on earth so that I can go to Heaven immediately?" Padre Pio replied: "By accepting everything from God's hands. By offering everything up to God with love and thanksgiving."

In another section of the book, Padre Pio writes, "Honesty and religion give us courage in every enterprise. They accompany us to the tomb where we go with a serene soul. I exhort you not to think of the health of the body, or wealth, but to think also of the spirit. Always be honest."

From his experiences with the souls in purgatory, Padre Pio taught that it is very easy to find forgiveness for sins while we are alive. While we are alive we can go to our brother or sister and ask for forgiveness. While we are alive we can choose to forgive those against whom we hold grudges or resentment. While we are alive, we can choose to love rather than to hate. While we are alive, it is easy to share rather than to hoard. Once we die, it is no longer so easy to rectify our earthly sins and transgressions. Padre Pio wrote, "It is better for us to do good now while we can, rather than suffer later on and desire to do something about it but are unable to do so."

Padre Pio taught that most souls go to purgatory. Most of us die with some unresolved issues from this life. For some souls, purgatory lasts but a few hours; for others it is for a few years; for still others the experience of purgatory may last for centuries.

I do not know what happens at death. Life is such a mystery. We enter this life as a mystery and we leave this life as a mystery. Most of us live our lives with some degree of denial as to the reality of our own impending death. I have come to believe in the existence of the soul and I have come to believe in the immortality of the soul. I do believe in a higher spiritual power that I know by the name of God. I do believe in the power of love in human relationships. I do not believe in an everlasting hell. But I have struggled with the notion of limited punishment or purgatory in the afterlife. After reading about the life and ministry of Padre Pio and learning about the degree to which the concept of purgatory is taught in other faith traditions, I must say that I find this concept plausible. It is not with fear that I embrace or consider the possibility of purgatory, rather it is with an increased intensity and focus as to what is really important in this life. What is really important is the spiritual. It is not important that I say that love is important, but I must be more loving. It is not important that I say forgiveness is important, but I must be more forgiving. It is not important that I say charity is important, but I must really learn to do unto others as I would like for them to do unto me. Would you not agree that love, forgiveness, and charity are the most important spiritual values by which a human being can live? Well, from a purgatorial perspective, why not learn and practice these truths now rather than risk having to learn these truths under much more difficult circumstances following human death?

The miracle of being alive is so precious, yet we often take it for granted. I hope I've given you something to think about this morning, even if you find the entire concept of purgatory absurd. Just remember: for most of the world and in most of the world's religious traditions, the concept of purgatory is anything but absurd. And for the early Universalists, the concept of purgatory was very much a part of Universalist theology. Think about it!

19

Lessons from a Pair of Crutches

I RECALL A READING from the theologian Matthew Fox in which he wrote that his pet dog was his best spiritual director and that some of his most profound theological insights came while spending time with his dog. Well, I want to share with you this morning that a pair of crutches can also teach spiritual lessons.

It was on Friday that I noticed some slight pain in my right knee as I climbed the stairways at the U.S. Army Medical Command building to head to the chaplain's office. It was the end of my first week of these five weeks of military duty. The following week I was slated to fill in for the command chaplain while he was on temporary duty out of state. Monday morning I was to attend the 7:30 a.m. commanders' conference. Tuesday morning I was slated to host a breakfast for all the senior chaplains stationed at Fort Sam Houston and Brooke Army Medical Center.

Well, Saturday morning around two o'clock. I awoke in my hotel suite to acute pain in my right knee. I could barely walk from my bed to the bathroom. I stayed awake the rest of the morning and I began administering ice packs to my knee. By eight o'clock the pain had subsided, but I decided to drive over to the Brooke Army Medical Center Emergency Department just to have the knee checked out. The fifteen-minute drive from my hotel to the emergency department was a bit difficult, but I managed OK. After a three-hour wait, I was finally seen by one of the physician assistants, also known as a "PA." X-rays were made of my knee, but they showed nothing out of the ordinary. The PA ordered an MRI for the following week and gave me prescriptions for both inflammation and pain. I asked her for a cane, but she said the hospital only provided crutches.

"I really don't need crutches," I protested.

"Well, take them with you anyway," she advised. "It is best to have them and not need them than to need them and not have them."

I walked out of the medical center carrying the crutches under my arm. When I got back to my hotel, I took the medicine for inflammation, but I did not take the pain medication. I really thought the worst was over.

"In the morning, I should be feeling great," I thought as I prepared for bed. "Maybe I'll even be back to running by Monday morning."

Around two o'clock Sunday morning I was again awakened with pain. This time the pain was much worse. Thank goodness one of the crutches was lying near my bed. I hobbled to the kitchen using the crutch as a cane. I looked and saw that my knee was now quite swollen and inflamed. I found the pain medication and quickly swallowed a pill. Next, I made an ice pack for the knee. However, neither the pain medication nor the ice pack seemed to help. At five o'clock that morning I called the emergency department. The PA who saw me on Saturday was not on duty. I described to the nurse what had happened with my knee. She advised me to come back over to the hospital.

"You don't understand," I said. "I can't bend my knee at all. There is no way I can get in my car and drive to the medical center."

She advised me to call an ambulance.

"Will the army pay for an ambulance to take me from my hotel to the medical center?" I asked.

"I don't know." She responded. "But if you have no other way to get here, an ambulance is your only option."

"Well, I don't want to take a chance on having to pay several hundred dollars for an ambulance ride to the medical center. I'll continue taking the medication and see if there is any improvement. If not, I will try and get a taxi to take me to the medical center," I explained. I thanked the nurse and hung up the phone.

"I can't believe this!" I pondered as I looked at my swollen knee. "Maybe if I take the medication and stay off the knee for a full day, the knee will recover. I don't have time to be sidelined by a sore knee."

For the rest of the day, I sat in a recliner with ice on my knee and I took both the inflammatory and pain medicine religiously. Whenever I had to move in my suite, I used both crutches to get me across the room. With sunrise, the pain seemed to lessen a bit, but with nightfall the pain returned. I came to realize that I probably would not be able to make it to the office Monday morning. I telephoned a subordinate chaplain and asked him if he could cover the early-morning meeting if my knee was no better by Monday morning. He agreed to cover the meeting.

Monday morning I was no better. I asked the hotel receptionist to call for a taxi van to take me to the medical center. Even with the van, it took me nearly five minutes to ease myself into a comfortable position in the back of the van. The drive to the medical center cost me thirty bucks. Again I waited for about three hours before being seen by a PA. This time the PA was male. He looked at my knee and said I needed to continue the medication and stay off my leg for two days. Now I realized I would miss the Tuesday breakfast that I was supposed to host. I just could not believe that I had become so handicapped so fast. Even with the crutches, I could now only barely move my right leg. I paid another thirty dollars for the taxi van to take me back to the hotel. I arranged for another chaplain to cover the Tuesday breakfast.

By Tuesday afternoon, the pain had subsided but the swelling remained. I was determined to make it to the office. I sat my alarm for three o'clock Wednesday morning. I knew I would need the extra time to shower, dress, and prepare for work. Everything takes so much longer when you are on crutches. It took me nearly thirty minutes just to figure out a way to get a sock over my right foot and lace my military boot. It is amazing what you can do with a coat hanger when you have to improvise. Using my crutches, I hobbled to my rental car in the hotel parking lot. With much effort, I tried to get into the driver's seat. With much pain, I managed to finally get both feet on the floorboard, but I found that I could not get my right foot on the brake pedal. I decided to try and drive the car using my left foot for the brake pedal and the right foot for the gas. I slowly backed out of my parking lot and found that I did not have the coordination for this sort of driving, especially considering the traffic and distance between the hotel and my office.

"This is too dangerous," I thought as I recalled the stress of driving in San Antonio traffic when my knee was well. I looked over at the hotel reception entrance in the distance.

"I'll go to the reception desk and call a taxi to get me to the office. Forget the extra expense! I will have to accept the fact that I am going to be dependent upon taxis and crutches until this knee recovers," I thought to myself as I pulled the crutches across my lap and onto the parking lot pavement. Slowly and carefully I used the crutches to help me exit the rental car.

It was at this point that I quit fighting with my injured knee. I decided I would use the crutches for as long as needed and that I would pay whatever the costs for taxis to take me where I needed to go. I decided to accept the fact that I was now a handicapped individual. It was at this point that the crutches and my injury took over the role of spiritual teacher. I hobbled to the hotel receptionist desk and telephoned for a taxi. The time was now about six thirty in the morning. To my surprise, the taxi arrived two minutes later. While riding in the taxi to my office, the taxi driver told me that six thirty to seven thirty in the morning were usually slow times for taxi drivers.

"We are busy from four thirty to five thirty in the morning taking folks to the airport, and we get busy again around seven thirty in the morning when we begin taking moms and their children to child care centers and to jobs," the taxi driver explained.

"You have those many mothers needing taxis to take children to child care and to get to jobs?" I asked rather puzzled.

"Oh, you would not believe how many folks are without a car. Some have cars that are in the repair shop. Others just can't afford the down payment and insurance to drive a car. For many single mothers, taxis are their only means of transportation."

I suddenly felt guilty over my earlier reluctance to spend part of my military salary on a taxi. I just never considered the fact that many folks have to travel by taxi every day to their jobs, and they were no doubt making much less than what I was earning as a military chaplain. I felt compassion for those who were so unfortunate, and I felt anger that I lived in a country where affordable public transportation is so lacking compared to the rest of the world.

When I arrived at my office, I made my way to my office. The crutches taught me about compassion and empathy. I was struck by the number of folks who opened doors for me and who offered to carry my brief case. Was it because I was a chaplain? Was it because I was in uniform? Was it because of my rank? Several individuals stopped me in the hallways and told me about their own knee and leg injuries.

I became aware of how most folks are in a hurry. With the crutches, I was moving at about twenty to twenty-five feet a minute. I was slow! I noticed how most folks seemed to speed by me. I would catch brief conversations as folks came from behind and soon left me far behind. I recalled a quote from Carl Jung: "Hurry is not of the devil, it is the devil!"

The crutches gave me a greater appreciation for nature. As I made my way from the Medical Command building to the Army Medical Center and School, I noticed a beautiful live oak tree near the walkway. I had walked this walkway many times before, but being in a hurry like everyone else, I had never noticed its beauty before. I discovered that a family of black birds and at least one squirrel lived in the branches of the tree. I became aware of many stunning cloud formations in the San Antonio area, and I even noticed the feeling of faint breezes upon my face. From the back of various taxicabs, I took time to observe some of the beautiful scenery in and around San Antonio and Fort Sam Houston.

Back at the hotel, I learned about kindness and lack of kindness. On three occasions, folks saw me coming and got in front of me so I would not delay them. Once it was at an elevator. I was about six feet from the elevator door when a man came from a side entrance and entered the elevator in front of me. At first I thought he might be hitting the button to keep the door opened for me, but I quickly learned that he was trying to get the door closed before I arrived. I guess he was in a hurry and did not have the time to wait the extra ten or fifteen seconds for me. The second time it was a woman who jumped in front of me as I was a few feet from the hotel's breakfast bar. The third time it was a woman who jumped in front of me as I was headed to the receptionist desk to call for a taxi. However, there were other men and women at the hotel who did hold doors open for me, who did hold elevators for me, and who offered to carry my brief case. I don't guess a few days are sufficient to warrant a random sample, but in all three hotel incidents when someone was in a hurry and got in front of me, they were Caucasian. In every instance in the hotel when folks showed kindness, they were either Hispanic or African American. I could not help but wonder if there was any significance to this observation, and if so, why?

I was able to discard the crutches after about eight days. I am now only using a cane. I can now drive my rental car again. I am still waiting for a final diagnosis from the MRI that I had last week. However, the purpose of this morning's message is not to complain or bore you regarding my knee injury. Rather, I wanted to share with you how much I learned about life and people from a pair of crutches. I suppose that almost any object or event can be a spiritual teacher when we allow ourselves to be receptive to divine truth speaking to us through the object or event. I am grateful for having to use crutches for eight days because the crutches taught me some truths about life that I might have otherwise missed.

The above homily was used as a morning devotional for U.S. Army Medical Command staff at Fort Sam Houston, Texas.

20

Finding Calm in the Midst of the Storm

A S YOU DESCEND ALONG many of the heavily traveled mountain roads in western North Carolina, you will often find signs identifying upcoming "runaway truck ramps." These inclined dirt ramps are usually fifty to a hundred yards in length and consist of several mounds of gravel or sand. The purpose of the ramp is to safely slow a runaway truck. If you are a trucker with a loaded trailer and lose your breaks going down one of those mountain highways, what a relief it must be to come upon one of these runaway truck ramps!

These are difficult times in which we live. Never in my life have I felt a greater passion for issues involving social action and social justice. At other times I am tempted to despair with feelings of hopelessness as I reflect upon the plight of America and our fragile planet. The same is true for many of you who are reading this article. It is easy to lose a sense of spiritual balance as we involve ourselves in the issues of social action and social justice. How can we maintain a sense of hope when our efforts seem to bring little or no positive results? Sometimes our lives feel like runaway trucks and we yearn for emotional and spiritual runaway truck ramps.

The late Catholic priest Anthony de Mello is one of my favorite spiritual writers. In *Taking Flight*, the last book he wrote prior to his death, de Mello gives the following illustration related to prayer: "There was an exhausted woodcutter who kept wasting time and energy chopping wood with a blunt axe because he did not have time, he said, to stop and sharpen the blade."

The well-known Quaker George Fox used to say, "Carry some quiet around inside thee. Be still and cool in thy own mind and spirit, from thy own thought, and then thou wilt feel the principle of God to turn thy mind to the Lord from whence cometh life; whereby thou may receive the strength and power to allay all storms and tempests."

I have found that my need for devotional time and prayer has increased as I exert more of my time and energy to issues related to social action and social justice. I need a spiritual discipline to help me feel balance and hope. Allow me to share with you one of my own spiritual discipline "runaway truck ramps." It was about six years ago when I began the discipline of beginning each morning with devotion and prayer.

Along with devotion and prayer, I have created a devotional altar within my home. My altar has grown over the years and now consists of religious icons and symbols from all over the world. I have statues of the Buddha from Korea, India, and Thailand; Catholic crucifixes from Hungary, Italy, and Mexico; a menorah from Jerusalem; a small replica of the Blue Mosque from Istanbul; and numerous Eastern Orthodox icons of Jesus and various saints from the Balkans and Eastern Europe. It is at my home altar that I keep my devotional book. For the past several years, my devotional book has been *The Imitation of Christ* by Thomas à Kempis. What a great little devotional book! Although I have read this book from cover to cover several times, the readings are always fresh and inspiring. When I travel, I pack a couple of the icons and my devotional book in my suitcase and I try and recreate a temporary small altar in my hotel or guest room.

I have found that having a special place in my home or room for devotion and prayer adds to the peace and tranquility I experience during the minutes I spend in spiritual reflection. When I sit in the chair adjacent to my home altar, a sense of calm comes over me. Even before I begin to read from my devotional book, my body seems to know that this is a sacred time and a sacred place. Beginning my day with prayer and devotion sets the tone for the rest of my day, and this practice helps me find a bit of calm in the midst of the storms associated with life and living.

How many of you use, or have used, a clock radio to wake you in the morning? Have you noticed how often in the day your mind goes back to the song that was playing when you were stirred from your morning sleep? Oftentimes, without even thinking about it, you will find yourself recalling the lyrics or the melody of the song. It is as if our minds are more receptive early in the morning for whatever it is we experience, hear, or read. I find the same is true with early morning devotions and prayer. During the day, my mind will often go back to the devotion I read in the morning, and like a planted seed, the wisdom of the morning devotional will often sprout and blossom into a deeper spiritual awareness as the day progresses.

We all need our emotional and spiritual runaway truck ramps. We all need a way to find a little calm in the midst of the storms of life. If you are not already beginning each day with some prayer and devotional time, I encourage you to consider trying this daily devotional discipline. I assure you that the ten to fifteen minutes you take for devotion and prayer in the morning will add so much more to the quality of the remaining hours of your day.

21

Healthy Skepticism

John 1:43–48

THE FOLLOWING READING FROM *Hymns for the Celebration of Life* was
written by the Unitarian Universalist minister Robert T. Weston and
is entitled "Cherish Your Doubts":

> Cherish your doubts, for doubt is the handmaiden of truth. Doubt
> is the key to the door of knowledge; it is the servant of discovery.
> A belief which may not be questioned binds us to error, for there
> is incompleteness and imperfection in every belief. Doubt is the
> touchstone of truth; it is an acid which eats away the false. Let no
> man fear for the truth, that doubt may consume it; for doubt is
> a testing of belief. The truth stands boldly and unafraid; it is not
> shaken by the testing. For truth, if it be truth, arises from each test-
> ing stronger, more secure. He that would silence doubt is filled with
> fear; the house of his spirit is built on shifting sands. But he that fears
> not doubt, and knows it use, is founded on a rock. He shall walk in
> the light of growing knowledge; the work of his hands will endure.
> Therefore let us not fear doubt, but let us rejoice in its help. It is to the
> wise as a staff to the blind; doubt it the handmaiden of truth.

In the scripture reading from John, we find a biblical character that
fits Robert Weston's description of an honest doubter. This story as recorded in the first chapter of John has no counterpart in any of the other
gospel stories. Nathanael is an ambiguous and obscure New Testament
character. He does not occur in the lists of the twelve disciples in the other
three gospels. Some biblical scholars believe him to be the same person as

Bartholomew who is mentioned in the Gospel of Mark. Nathanael's most famous utterance is his skeptical question when Philip enthusiastically told him about Jesus. Nathanael's response was, "Can anything good come out of Nazareth?"

We see in Nathanael's response that Nathanael was neither naive nor gullible. Perhaps Nathanael had heard of many other individuals who claimed to be the Messiah. So what? Nathanael's response is similar to what perhaps many of you might think when you hear of a new program coming out of Congress or the White House. "Can anything good come out of Washington?" Nathanael, for whatever reason, appears to be a rather skeptical individual. Nathanael is the sort of individual that would probably feel at home in a Universalist congregation. After all, many of you came to Universalism and Unitarian Universalism because of your reluctance to accept hook, line, and sinker the orthodox Christian doctrine that is preached in many of our neighboring churches. You wanted the freedom to question.

So when Nathanael comments, "Can anything good come out of Nazareth?" Philip merely tells him to check it out: "Come and see," he suggests to the skeptical Nathanael. And Nathanael does go with Philip to see Jesus, perhaps with the fragile hope that this man Jesus, indeed, would be different from the many would-be messiahs of his time. The fact that Nathanael does agree to go with Philip to meet Jesus is important for this shows that Nathanael's skepticism has not crossed into cynicism. With skepticism one is still open to the truth, but with cynicism one has given up on there being any truth. So Nathanael meets this man Jesus, and to Nathanael's surprise Jesus compliments him for his honest skepticism. Jesus says to Nathanael, "Here is a real Israelite; there is nothing false in him!"

In what Jesus says to Nathanael we find Jesus affirming that honest doubting and human skepticism are healthy. Spiritual claims need to be examined, impressions need to be tested, and truth needs to be proven. We also find in this passage of scripture Jesus affirming the value of authenticity and being genuine.

A Jewish parable reports a disciple saying to his rabbi, "I am troubled with uncertainty about God and there are times when my faith is weak."

"Don't worry too much," counseled the rabbi, "and return home in peace. For so long as you are worried about your faith, all is well. The time to be concerned is when you no longer have feelings of doubt."

It seems to be that as human beings we are all born questioners. Consider the wonderment of a little child in his or her eyes before the child can speak. If there is any word that is spoken with more frequency than any other word by little children, that word must be *why*. Every child is full of every kind of question, about every kind of thing that moves, and shines, and changes, in the little world in which he or she lives. That is the basic or rudimentary skepticism in human nature. And having observed puppies, kittens, and various other animal creatures during their early development, I can't help but wonder if some of this basic skepticism transcends human nature. Most young animals seem curious by nature. But for the human child, it is an inevitable thing to question. Questioning is our basic means of learning, a means of exploring that can lead one onward and upward into ever new experiences and to a fullness of life.

To listen to some versions of Christianity preached from more fundamental church pulpits, as well as some of the television evangelists we hear on Sunday morning television, we might assume that when Jesus summoned his disciples he was looking for a bunch of nonthinking robot-like persons who would travel with him and accept whatever he said without any questions. But in this passage of scripture we see that this is not the case. Here we find that Jesus saw in the healthy skepticism of Nathanael an open and searching integrity. "Here," Jesus said when Philip brought Nathanael to check him out, "is a real Israelite; there is nothing false about him!"

In 1929, the Seventh-day Adventist Church expelled from its membership a Bulgarian immigrant named Victor Houteff. Houteff became obsessed with passages in the book of Ezekiel describing how the angel of God divided the faithful from the sinful before the fall of Jerusalem to the Babylonians. Houteff established a splinter congregation in 1935 on the outskirts of Waco, Texas. When Houteff died in 1955, his widow led the sect. She predicted that the end of the world would happen in 1959. When it didn't, she dissolved the sect. Some members stayed on, however, and called themselves the "Branch Davidians."

A young man named Vernon Howell joined them in 1984 and soon took over the group and its compound. In 1990, Howell changed his name to David Koresh (Koresh is Hebrew for Cyrus, the sixth-century BC king of Persia). He was indeed a prophet, for he preached that the destiny of the Branch Davidians was to perish in a fiery Armageddon. It appears that the United States government was accommodating enough to play out the role that Koresh had assigned it.

The world has always been a fertile ground for strange religious formations. But what happened at Waco—and similarly, at Jonestown before it—makes us wonder how some people can so blindly and unquestioningly follow such strange prophets as a Koresh or a Jim Jones, even to their deaths. Why didn't they investigate the peculiar ways of these paranoid and morally corrupt men bent on self-destruction? How could they be fooled and manipulated into actually helping to create the inferno and mass suicide such evil brought about? We pity them all, as well as the many yet living who have the same nonquestioning attitude and are vulnerable to false prophets and messiahs waiting in the wings.

John Ciardi wrote in a recent issue of *The Saturday Review* that it is important to have the courage of your convictions, and it is equally important to have the courage of your confusions. He said, "Show me a person who is not confused and I will show you one who is not thinking."

Personally, I will confess that I feel very uncomfortable when I am in a conversation with someone who seems to be certain about everything. I am also uncomfortable in a worship service or a funeral when the minister conveys this same certainness in discussing God, death, and eternal life. As I shared in a previous sermon, so much of religion is mystery. And there is very little that we can say with certainty about mystery.

In 1887, the English minister Henry Drummond wrote a sermon entitled "Dealing with Doubt." I want to share with you a few paragraphs from that sermon. He wrote:

> The world is a sphinx. It is a vast riddle . . . an unfathomable mystery. In every leaf, in every cell of every leaf, there are a hundred problems. There are ten good years of a person's life in investigating what is a leaf, and there are five good years more in investigating the things that are in the things that are in the leaf. It seems the world has been planned to incite investigative activity.
>
> The instrument with which we attempt to investigate the world is impaired. Some say it fell, and the glass is broken. Some say prejudice, heredity, or sin have spoiled its sight, and have blinded our eyes and deadened our ears. In any case the instruments with which we work upon truth, even in the strongest minds, are feeble and inadequate to their tremendous task.
>
> It must be said, as well, that even religious truth is doubtable. There is no absolute proof for any of it. Even that fundamental proof, the

existence of a god, no one can prove by reason. The ordinary proof for the existence of God involves either an assumption, argument in a circle, or a contradiction. The impression of God is kept up by experience, not by logic.

What does this teach us? It teaches us great intellectual humility. It teaches us sympathy and toleration with all people who venture upon the ocean of truth to find a way through it for themselves. The Church has erred in this area. In the past it has said: "There is a heretic. Burn him!" We have got past that physically; have we got past it morally? What do we say to a skeptical person today? Not "Burn him!" but "Brand him!" "Brand him!" Call him a name. A "liberal," an "agnostic," a "humanist."

Contrast Christ's treatment of skeptics . . . like Nathanael, or Thomas. Rather than condemn, scold, or ostracize, he accepted their search and their struggle. We know of his strange partiality for the outsiders . . . for the scattered heretics up and down the country; of the care with which he loved to deal with them, and of the respect in which he held their difficulties of belief. Investigation is can't yet believe; unbelief is won't believe. Investigation is looking for light; unbelief is content with darkness. Loving darkness rather than light . . . that is what Christ attacked. But for the intellectual questioning of Thomas, and Philip, and Nathanael, and Nicodemus, he was respectful and generous and tolerant.

What a profound Universalist sermon, and to think it was preached in 1887 by a trinitarian and evangelistic minister in the Free Church of England. I can't help but wonder if Henry Drummond ever considered becoming Universalist?

King Stanislaus I of Poland once said, "To believe with certainty, we must begin with doubting." And it was Alfred Tennyson who wrote, "There lives more faith in honest doubt, believe me, than in half the creeds."

When Albert Einstein was asked how he hit on the theory of relativity, he replied, "I challenged an axiom." It was by investigating what others took for granted that Einstein developed a new view of reality.

The philosopher Bertrand Russell once said, "It's healthy now and then to hang a question mark on things you've long taken for granted."

"Jesus was a magnificent doubter," wrote Harry Emerson Fosdick, and he gave some examples of things Jesus doubted. For instance, there were ideas about a war-making messiah who would overthrow the Roman occupation force in Israel, but Jesus doubted that image of messiahship. People said that "an eye for an eye and a tooth for a tooth" was the true law of human relations, but Jesus doubted that. Many believed that long prayers, rigid Sabbath laws, and dietary laws were essential for genuine religion, but Jesus doubted that. Some persons traced personal suffering back to some supposed personal sin, but Jesus doubted such neat explanations.

Is there any surprise that Jesus, the doubter, found respect for those of his disciples who also were doubters? Jesus knew that honest doubts, fully faced, frankly explored, will lead inevitably to truth.

One beauty of Universalism is that we can affirm the doubters among us. We realize that honest skepticism is healthy and can only lead to a deeper and more profound faith.

Cherish your doubts, for they are, indeed, the handmaidens of truth.

22

God's Abundance

Matthew 6:25–33

IN THE SCRIPTURE READING from Matthew we are admonished to "look at the birds of the air: they neither sow nor reap nor gather into barns, and yet your heavenly Father feeds them."

As are many of you, I am fascinated by birds. Since moving to the Outlaw's Bridge parsonage, I've installed two bird feeders adjacent to living room windows so I can sit and watch the various birds that come to feed. As a child, I was often fascinated by birds. I suppose my earliest fascination with birds surrounded their ability to fly. Birds have a freedom of movement that is impossible for us earthbound beings. The ability to fly from one place to another with seemingly effortless ease is much to be envied. It was no doubt humanity's envy of birds that led to our first airplane—and if you look at some of the earliest designs for human flying machines, those designs resembled birds. Secondly, there is the music of birds. No other creatures, except human beings, are able to make musical sound.

However, a third fascination that I've come to have of birds is that they seem to be free of the responsibilities people have. It often seems that birds are provided for with minimal work and a complete absence of worry or fear for the future. This complete absence of worry or fear for the future is no doubt related to Jesus' words in Matthew.

A blue jay one day showed me that not all birds are like the birds described by Jesus, and in this particular blue jay's behavior, I believe I received an insight into one of humanity's obstacles to fully enjoying what is called God's abundance.

During my high school days my father built a bird feeder and placed it within view of our dining room window. Often during breakfast and evening meals we were entertained by the large number and variety of different birds that visited the feeder for a snack. I can recall seeing at times four or five birds sitting at the feeder while another half dozen or so sat perched in the limbs of nearby trees awaiting their turn at the feeder.

It was either I or one of my two younger brothers, Thomas or Joseph, who would refill the feeder with additional birdseed whenever the birds neared depleting their supply. Thus, regardless of how many birds visited the feeder each day, there was always an abundance of food.

Several weeks passed, and we noticed that the birds using the feeder decreased to almost none. The feeder needed filling only about once a week, whereas before we had refilled the feeder at least every other day.

At first we thought that we had perhaps gotten a batch of poor quality birdseed. However, Joseph, my youngest brother, spent several hours one afternoon observing the feeder and in the course of that afternoon he discovered the real reason for the decreased usage.

A blue jay had taken over the feeder as his property and was now the only bird using the feeder. The blue jay would feed and then sit in a nearby tree, rising to attack any bird that approached "his" feeder. Guard duty occupied his every waking hour, and the only time another bird got to use the feeder was when the blue jay had momentarily gone to chase away some other bird.

The blue jay taught us a lesson. By assuming ownership of the feeder, the blue jay forfeited its freedom. The blue jay was no longer free to come and go at will for the blue jay was tied to the work of guarding the feeder. The blue jay was possessed by its possessions. If it is possible for a bird to experience worry or fear, no doubt this blue jay experienced some of both. And out of the blue jay's fear that other birds would exhaust the supply of food in the feeder, the blue jay actually decreased the amount of birdseed that we placed in the feeder. It was the blue jay's action that diminished the amount of food available for all the birds who visited the feeder.

We three boys ran the blue jay away by throwing small stones at it whenever the blue jay appeared near the feeder. Eventually, the other birds returned to the feeder, and we went back to having to refill the feeder every other day.

People often do the same thing that the blue jay did. We, too, can become possessed by our possessions, and by our actions restrict the flow of supply into our lives.

Like the blue jay, when we restrict the demand for good in our lives, we reduce the supply. When we believe that the supply of good is limited, we restrict the use of that good, less is available, and the anticipated short supply comes about.

A few years ago, Johnny Carson joked on the *Tonight Show* about an upcoming shortage of toilet tissue. In the coming weeks, a national toilet tissue shortage actually occurred. Out of fear, folks began purchasing more tissue than they needed, and as the rumor spread, grocery store shelves were depleted. Our prophecy of short supply becomes self-fulfilling. I suspect that this is true both spiritually as well as physically.

We are a planet of over four billion people—two-thirds of whom are inadequately fed or starving, while the other one-third are dieting. What is more distressing is that although a majority of the world lacks sufficient food, in actuality there is sufficient food in the world that every human being could be adequately fed if the world's food was shared.

Indeed we are a lot like the blue jay.

Jesus said, "Therefore do not be anxious, saying, what shall we eat? or what shall we drink? or what shall we wear? For the Gentiles seek all these things; and your heavenly Father knows that you need them all. But seek first his kingdom and his righteousness, and all these things shall be yours as well."

That which is called "God's abundance" is all about us. We can't possess this abundance, we can only share it. And the more we share of this abundance, the greater will be the supply. This includes smiles and love.

The scripture teaches us to tithe. This means that we should give ten percent to charity. I have since learned that in all the major religions of the world there are similar teachings about giving.

Fifteen years ago I resented this teaching. I thought of this as a tricky way to get naive and trusting folks to give money to churches. I have since made a 180-degree turn in my thought. I now believe that this teaching represents a universal spiritual law. I now believe that much of the world's problems would be solved and most of the earth's inhabitants would be so much happier if they learned the secret of giving. True giving blesses both the giver and the receiver.

In 2 Corinthians 9:7 we read that "God loves a cheerful giver." I want to challenge you to give away at least ten percent of your income. Just try it. Don't give it all to church. Divide it among charities and causes that you genuinely believe in. Try it for three months and see what happens. I think you will be pleasantly surprised.

PART TWO

Reflections

23

Lessons from an Oak Leaf

I WAS SITTING ON the porch of the Outlaw's Bridge Universalist Church parsonage, notebook in hand, preparing next Sunday's sermon. It was a beautiful autumn afternoon. With each gentle breeze, numerous leaves came floating to earth from the branches of a nearby oak tree. From the corner of my eye, I caught a glimpse of one leaf as it drifted onto the porch and came to rest beside my chair. I reached down and lifted the leaf by its tiny stem. Bringing it closer, I forgot my sermon preparation and instead enjoyed a natural curiosity as I examined this leaf for a few minutes.

In a few places there remained splotches of autumn orange, but the predominant color of the leaf was brown. Gone was the green. The veins remained clearly visible, arching out from the stem. And from these veins were smaller veins, and from these—even smaller ones. Not only did these veins support the blade, but they were once the means by which the leaf transported vital nutrients and water to its tissues.

The life was gone from this leaf, yet the remnant of what that leaf had been during its life remained clearly visible. I held in my hand the legacy of what was once a living leaf. Where is the life that was once the leaf? All that remains is the legacy of that life.

Shifting the position of the leaf to reflect the glare of the afternoon sun, the lifeless veins became even more prominent. Each vein remains as it was during life.

Perhaps it is the same for human life. Where is the life that was once a person? Yet after our deaths, the events, excitements, influences, loves, joys, tragedies, struggles, and sorrows of that life remain as clear memories for those with whom we shared our life's journey. Our life remains clear for those who remember. Memories are like the veins in the lifeless leaf.

After our deaths, we have no influence over the memories others will have of our lives. Like the leaf, what remains is the legacy of our lives. Indeed, our life is an open book in the collective memories of all with whom we once had contact.

I arose from my chair, gently carrying this brown oak leaf into the front yard. I placed the leaf among a multitude of other leaves. I returned to the porch and continued writing my sermon.

November 1991.

24

Coincidence or a Father's Final Gift?

IT WAS MONDAY AFTERNOON, November 8, 1993. I was sitting in my office at the Wayne County Mental Health Center in Goldsboro, North Carolina. On my desk were several stacks of client records I was trying to complete for transfer to other therapists. I had been supplementing my part-time parish ministry income by working as a counselor at this mental health facility.

This was to be my final week at Wayne County Mental Health Center. Most of my remaining work involved client record keeping. I was scheduled to begin a new job as a chaplain with the South Carolina Department of Corrections the following week.

It seems that I rather suddenly became extremely sleepy that afternoon. I just could not seem to keep my eyes open. Finally, I closed my office door and decided to risk a short nap. Although I had occasionally taken a five-to-ten-minute nap during my one-hour lunch break, this would be my first and only attempt to risk a short nap during working hours. I only intended to sleep a few minutes.

Moments later I was in the midst of a most vivid dream. The characters in the dream were animated in cartoon fashion. My focus in the dream was upon a crippled grasshopper slowly moving along a highway. The grasshopper appeared to be weak and dying.

The sickly grasshopper made a few short movements and then it fell still upon the highway pavement. As I observed the motionless grasshopper, my attention was drawn to an electrical power line running adjacent to the highway. Sitting upon the power line was a very colorful and vibrant bumblebee. The bumblebee appeared to be smiling at me. Immediately, it occurred to me that what had been the grasshopper was now the bumblebee.

"So, this is what happens at death." I reflected as I continued to dream. "At death, we simply take on a different form and body."

As soon as I recognized the meaning of the dream, I was suddenly awakened. The vividness of the dream was unusual. The simple message of the dream was profound.

"What a strange dream!" I thought as I recalled the animated cartoon caricature of the smiling bumblebee looking toward me from atop the power line. I tried to remember what had preceded the crippled grasshopper in my dream, but I could not recall any memory prior to that of seeing the old crippled grasshopper slowly dying on the highway pavement.

As I sat at my office desk reflecting upon this unusual dream, I felt an urge to telephone my father. Remembering that I had talked with my father the previous Saturday, I decided against trying to call him. The previous Saturday's telephone conversation had been one of our best telephone visits in years. My father had just returned to his Lake Greenwood home after a week's vacation at Myrtle Beach, South Carolina. We talked about his health. My father's health had deteriorated over the past two years due to heart and kidney disease. With much excitement, I told him about the Victorian house I was in the process of purchasing in the small town of Clio, South Carolina. He had shared my enthusiasm. He was looking forward to making a trip to see me as soon as I was settled into my new job as a prison chaplain.

Instead of telephoning my father, I decided to place a call to my mother. My mother and father divorced in 1982 after thirty-two years of marriage. The bitterness and hurt that marked their separation and divorce had given way to forgiveness. During the past several years, they both spoke with concern and caring for the other during my visits in their respective homes.

As I retrieved my MCI calling card from my wallet, I realized that calling my mother from work was really out of character for me. Rarely did I make a personal long-distance call prior to five o'clock in the afternoon unless it was an emergency. But I decided to call her anyway.

"Hello!" It was my mother's voice on the other end of the line.

"Hey, Mom, this is Vernie. Don't be alarmed. I know this is an odd time to be calling, but I had a few minutes and I just wanted to give you a call."

My mother and I visited for several minutes over the phone. Neither one of us had any major news to share with the other.

It was later that evening that I would learn of my father's death. Frances, my stepmother, was driving my father to a four o'clock medical appointment when he died. Apparently, his death was rather sudden and without pain. Frances became alarmed when my father dropped the bottles of medicine he had been carrying in his lap. He appeared to be sleeping. When he failed to respond to her shouts and her attempts to shake his shoulder, Frances used their cellular phone to notify the highway patrol that they were driving directly to the hospital. Attempts to revive my father on the emergency room ramp were unsuccessful. My father was pronounced dead a few minutes after arriving at Self Memorial Hospital in Greenwood, South Carolina.

My first reaction was acute grief. It was later the next day that I recalled the vivid dream on the afternoon of my father's death. Was my dream a coincidence, or might it have been something more? I could not remember what time it was when I took my brief nap. It might have been as early as 3 p.m. or as late as 4 p.m. However, I did know that the call to my mother was within two or three minutes of waking from my nap. My father became unconscious in the car sometime between 3:30 p.m. and 3:50 p.m.

It was several weeks later when I received the MCI telephone bill indicating the time of my call to my mother. Meanwhile, I asked Frances to send me the time of her call to the highway patrol when her cellular phone bill arrived. When I finally was able to compare the recorded times for the two calls, I was shocked.

There was only one minute of time between the two phone calls. The call to the highway patrol was at 3:43 p.m., and the call to my mother was at 3:44 p.m. It was obvious that my vivid dream of the dying grasshopper and the smiling bumblebee took place as my father was dying.

Coincidence or not, the dream has come to have a very special meaning for me. Immortality of the human soul was the message of the dream. I've come to believe that the dream and its message were my father's final gift to his eldest son.

25

Gardening as Sacramental Theology

I HAVE FOUND GARDENING to be a source of much joy, pleasure, and satisfaction. This summer's garden is my largest ever, with several rows of corn, three varieties of squash, tomatoes, peppers, lettuce, collards, cantaloupes, watermelons, and even pumpkins. It is exciting to watch the plants grow, and nothing tastes better than vegetables from your own garden. During many an evening I have become oblivious to time and daily concerns as I crawled among the rows of crops pulling weeds from my garden. I have become acquainted with several garden snails that live in my garden and I've been fascinated and frightened by numerous other small creatures (to include a black snake) that frequent the plot.

Not only does gardening bring creativity to the tended soil, but also in the act of gardening the mind of the gardener finds renewed creativity. Whether tilling the soil, planting the seed, observing the young sprout, pruning an excess plant, removing a weed, watching a bee buzz from blossom to blossom, or harvesting the crop—there can be witnessed the mirror reflection of human glory, suffering, joy, and pain. The act of gardening stimulates the power of daydreaming, and in my imagination I sometimes perceive human characteristics, tragedy, and virtue among the various plants and each one's course of life. I have beheld the randomness of illness and injury due to other creatures and disease. There is the joy and hope displayed by a damaged plant that recovers and produces a yield equal to or greater than its siblings. Then there are those few plants that seem to be off to such a great start only to later produce an inferior crop. A garden plot is a magnificent theatrical display with the dance of God interposed in each day's performance.

During one afternoon's daydreaming, it occurred to me that the act of gardening can have parallels with religious ritual and sacrament.

Augustine of Hippo embraced the theory that sacraments are a means by which interior meanings are expressed by one agent to another. In other words, in a sacrament the sense of the divine presence may be more intensely conveyed in the act of the ritual than in the verbal communication about the divine reality. Might gardening serve as a sacrament for a creation-centered spirituality? Perhaps the answer lies in the eyes and faith of the gardener. It is interesting to note how frequently Jesus made reference to gardens, crops, pruning, and harvesting in discussing the kingdom of God. In the fifteenth chapter of John, Jesus uses the term "gardener" to metaphorically describe the activity of God in human lives.

There is an added dimension of sacrament to my own garden plot. My garden is located behind the Outlaw's Bridge Universalist Church parsonage adjacent to what was once a small barn. I have learned from parishioners that my garden plot is on the same ground as were the gardens of several other Universalist ministers of years gone by. It was one evening as I was making rhythmic strokes with my hoe that I suddenly envisioned those former ministers standing where I was standing and doing what I was doing. A sense of peace and calm pervaded my entire body. For a brief moment I was at one (at-one-ment) with the hoe, the garden, and my world. The experience was for me a sacred one.

Perhaps the spirituality of Universalism is related to the fact that most Universalist churches originated in rural areas. There does seem to be a natural spirituality in rural life and living that is difficult to find in the concrete, noise, hustle, and bustle of city life. Whether consciously perceived or not, perchance the sacrament of gardening has for many Universalists added to their experience and understanding of that which we call God.

Does gardening as sacrament sound like strange theology? In the biblical story of creation remember that it was God who planted the first garden (Genesis 1) and made it home. It should not surprise even the most fundamentalist of Christians that God would still find a home in a backyard garden plot.

June 1990.

26

Honoring Our Unitarian Universalist Veterans

VETERANS DAY, ORIGINALLY ESTABLISHED as Armistice Day in 1926, is the official holiday when the United States honors our men and women who are veterans. The holiday was renamed Veterans Day in 1954 to honor all U.S. veterans.

Recognizing and honoring the military service of members in our Unitarian Universalist congregations are not high priorities for many of our churches and fellowships. But there are literally hundreds of Unitarian Universalists in our nation's armed forces today, and chances are that someone sitting near you on Sunday morning was once in uniform.

I suspect that many Unitarian Universalist veterans feel some awkwardness in sharing this distinction with other UUs on Veterans Day. Given the number of veterans who are members of our religious faith, I can't help wishing our Veterans Day observances were different.

Our veterans' military experiences are varied. Some enjoyed peacetime service. Others were touched by the horrors of combat. A few continue to carry physical and emotional scars from their wartime service. For some veterans, it was their military experience that initiated the religious search that eventually brought them to Unitarian Universalism. I know a few current and former military personnel who actually discovered Unitarian Universalism while in uniform. After all, we have UU chaplains in all branches of military service, and a few of our larger military installations have UU congregations that meet in military chapels.

Political opinions vary among those in uniform as it does among civilians. One big difference for our men and women in uniform is that they do not have the same freedom to express their opinions publicly as do other citizens. The tempo of military deployments today places a great strain on our military personnel and their families. I have friends and colleagues who are on their second one-year deployment in less than four years.

On this Veterans Day weekend, I encourage Unitarian Universalists to honor the veterans and military personnel in their congregations. Regardless of your political views regarding the wars in Iraq and Afghanistan, our members of the armed forces do not start wars nor do they dictate foreign policy.

Our Unitarian Universalist military personnel need your support and your love. Expressing that support could be as simple as lighting a candle for your veterans on Sunday morning. Or you might consider offering time in your worship service for individual veterans to stand and share a special memory or lesson in life that was gained from military service. Hearing what our Unitarian Universalist veterans have to say and share just might be more powerful than any sermon preached from your congregation's pulpit!

This year, when you see Veterans Day flags flying in your towns, no matter what your feelings are about this or any war, my fondest hope is that you will remember our UU veterans and UU military personnel. Remember them and reach out to them in love, extending the olive branch of acceptance and respect that our UU faith calls us to embrace each day.

The above reflection was written in October 2006 and was posted on the Unitarian Universalist Association web page. It has since been reprinted in numerous Unitarian Universalist newsletters and read in various Unitarian Universalist worship services in recognition of Veterans Day.

27

On Desert Storm Celebrations

I WRITE THIS REFLECTION in late June 1991. Here in eastern North Carolina yellow ribbons and American flags remain prominently displayed on houses, businesses, city streets, and churches. Desert Storm victory celebrations continue throughout the nation. Although I applaud America's support for our men and women in uniform, there are aspects of these so-called patriotic events that disturb me. Writing in the June 17 issue of *Army Times*, Sergeant Major (Ret.) Shelby T. Clark calls the public and official reactions to the Persian Gulf War "downright scary." Stating that the "nation has gone a bit berserk in praise and idolatry," Clark goes on to compare aspects of this Desert Storm patriotic hysteria with Adolf Hitler's Nuremberg rallies. The retired Sergeant Major's language is harsh, but perhaps there is some truth in his observations.

During my four months of Desert Storm related army chaplaincy duty, I witnessed numerous "victory" and/or "welcome home" celebrations. There was the tearful joy of witnessing families and couples reunited. There was the feeling of genuine patriotic pride in listening to the local army band play the national anthem while returning soldiers stood in formation and saluted the American flag. But as I looked into the eyes of many within the crowd and listened to their conversations, I felt some uneasiness. For some there was a healthy patriotism and a genuine welcoming home attitude. Yet I detected something else. I felt emptiness in many of the conversations. It was as though the patriotic fervor was an attempt to soothe some inner pain. Maybe some of this relates to Vietnam, but I have come to suspect that the real malady stems from the average American's desperate need for meaning and purpose. The vast majority of the Desert Storm warriors came from the families of lower- and lower-middle-class Americans. Desert Storm gave to many poor and struggling

American families the illusion of meaning and purpose. Having a relative in uniform gave an ascribed status to every family member.

Another troubling aspect of our Desert Storm celebrations is the glorification of war. War is horrible and is never good. Of course, I am grateful for the remarkable low casualties among the forces of the United Nations, but I grieve the feeling of loss due to the deaths of so many Iraqis.

Worse than war is to live and die devoid of meaning and purpose. A tragedy in the Gulf War was that so many of the Iraqi soldiers who died in battle did not believe in the Iraqi cause, that is, Saddam Hussein's cause. Many who wore the Iraqi uniform did so from fear of execution should they refuse. There is tragedy in the meaninglessness with which many individual Iraqi soldiers met death.

America's Desert Storm celebrations resemble the festivities surrounding sporting events. Our celebrations ignore the horror, sadness, and tragedy of the Gulf War.

It is from the ancient religion of Taoism that we can find guidance as to the proper behavior for those victorious in war. In the *Tao Te Ching* it is written:

> When great numbers of people are killed, one should weep over them with sorrow. When victorious in war, one should observe the rites of mourning.

There is no such thing as a good war. In an imperfect world, perhaps war is sometimes the lesser of evils. But war remains evil. History will determine the relative "rightness" of Desert Storm. In the meantime, may we observe a healthy mourning for the many dead as a result of this war.

June 1991.

28

A Visit to Dachau

THERE IS SOMETHING MYSTERIOUS and a bit haunting about a prison yard. It is as if the very ground within the brick walls and razor or barbed wire fences somehow absorbs the emotions and feelings of those who have spent time walking those yards. I spent eight years employed as a correctional chaplain at two prisons in North Carolina and two prisons in South Carolina. I worked as a mental health counselor at prisons in Alabama and South Carolina. I even spent a weekend of training at California's notorious San Quentin Prison. I've visited many other prisons. At every prison I've ever worked or visited during my employment as a correctional chaplain, I found time to "walk the yard." Many inmates and staff thought I walked the yard for exercise, and that is partially true. However, I discovered that some of my best counseling was possible while walking the yard. Often, inmates were more open to sharing and talking with me when walking the yard than when sitting in my office. Some inmates would approach me on the yard who would never approach me in my chapel office. Sometimes I walked the yard alone while waiting for an inmate or inmates to join me. It was while walking alone that I sometimes sensed the despair, fear, hopelessness, and loneliness that emanated from the ground of the prison yard. Was it my imagination or was it something real?

I visited the infamous Dachau Concentration Camp with soldiers from the U.S. Army Garrison in Darmstadt, Germany, in April 2008. Dachau is about a four-hour drive by bus from Darmstadt. Dachau Concentration Camp was the first regular concentration camp established by the Nazi government. It was noted as the first concentration camp for political prisoners. The prison was located on the grounds of an abandoned munitions factory near the town of Dachau, about ten miles northwest of Munich in southern Germany.

Initially, the prison held internees consisting of German Communists, Social Democrats, trade unionists, and other political opponents of the Nazi regime. Later other groups were imprisoned at Dachau, including Jehovah's Witnesses, Roma (Gypsies), homosexuals, and any repeat criminal offenders. There were very few Jewish prisoners at Dachau during the first few years of its existence. However, with the increased persecution of Jews, the population of Jewish prisoners became more pronounced. In 1938, over 10,000 Jewish men were interned in Dachau. Among the many Jewish men who were held in Dachau was the psychiatrist Viktor Frankl, who later wrote his classic *Man's Search for Meaning*, which is primarily based upon his experiences as a concentration camp prisoner.

The Dachau camp was a training center for SS concentration camp guards, and Dachau's organization and routine became a model for all Nazi concentration camps. The prison was divided into two sections: the camp area, which included the prison yard, and the crematoria area. The camp area consisted of thirty-two barracks, including one for clergy imprisoned for their opposition to the Nazi government and one barracks reserved for medical experiments. The courtyard between the prison and the central kitchen was used for the summary execution of prisoners. An electrified barbed wire fence, a ditch, and a wall with seven guard towers surrounded the camp. The towers were manned 24/7 with armed guards. Many survivors report that attempting to cross the fence and ditch was a common method of suicide since it was impossible to climb the wall without being shot by one of the tower guards.

The medical experiments conducted at Dachau included high-altitude ones using a decompression chamber, malaria and tuberculosis experiments, hypothermia experiments, and the testing of new medications. Dachau prisoners were also forced to test methods of making seawater potable (forced drinking of various degrees of salty water) and of halting excessive bleeding after using knives to slice the arteries and veins of inmates. Hundreds of inmates died or were permanently disabled as a result of these experiments. Most other inmates were used as forced laborers under harsh working conditions that resulted in their deaths. The crematorium was built so that the bodies of those inmates who were executed or who died from experiments, torture, or forced labor could be burned to ashes without the citizens of nearby Dachau really knowing the extent to which death and killing were taking place in the facility. Outside the crematorium are mounds of dirt consisting of the ashes of thousands of Dachau human bodies.

During my tour of the former concentration camp, I took some time alone to walk what had been the prison yard at Dachau. As I walked the gravel yard, I felt something vaguely familiar. Was it my imagination, or did those prison grounds still carry some of the emotional pain of those who suffered there?

If you have never read Frankl's *Man's Search for Meaning*, I recommend it to you. Even in the misery and suffering of a place like Dachau, Frankl discovered that he was able to exercise the most important freedom of all, which is the freedom to determine one's own attitude and spiritual well-being. No one can take away your soul unless you allow that person to do so. Most humans can endure any suffering if they can find meaning and hope despite their suffering and pain. Frankl found that a strength he used to fight to stay alive and not lose hope was to think of his wife. Frankl observed that it was those in the concentration camps who had nothing to live for who died the quickest.

One of the most haunting memories of my visit to Dachau was my tour of the museum housed in the same building that was used to process new arrivals. Walking though the museum, I read and saw photos of some of the torture that took place in the prison. I learned that much torture took place in the very buildings that are now used as the museum. New arrivals were often brutalized to the point that they committed suicide their first night at Dachau rather than risk another day of torture.

It has been approximately ten months since my visit to Dachau. Although I promised the editor of the *Universalist Herald* to write an article about Dachau, I have struggled with the issue of torture and how to address torture in describing my visit. By the spring of 2008, it was common knowledge that the Bush/Cheney White House had sanctioned torture in such places as Abu Ghraib, the Guantanamo Bay prison, and various CIA-run secret prisons. Not only was torture sanctioned, but many of the detainees tortured by U.S. personnel were later found to be innocent of terrorist charges. Many made false confessions as a result of torture. Yes, I was sickened by what I read and saw in the Dachau museum, but an aspect of my discomfort was the awareness that my own country had now embraced torture. Even more disturbing for me was discovering that many of my relatives and friends seem to think that there is nothing wrong with torture as a tool in our so-called Global War on Terror.

It is true that most of the torture techniques used by the post-9/11 United States were not the same techniques used at Dachau. We have not used detainees in painful medical experiments. We did not build crematoriums to dispose of victims. However, water boarding (simulated drowning), extreme sleep deprivation, exposing detainees to extremes in temperature, forcing male internees to perform sex acts in front of female soldiers, and smearing the feces from one detainee over the face of another detainee are all considered forms of torture by most of the civilized world. Torture is torture! Furthermore, experienced interrogators will vouch for the fact that information gained from torture is rarely reliable. Several post-9/11 detainees have died as a result of U.S. torture. It was a relief to me that both the McCain and Obama campaigns ran on platforms to end U.S. torture of detainees and to close the international embarrassment of the Guantanamo Bay prison in Cuba. And now that Barack Obama is officially president of the United States, it appears that serious effort is now underway to close the Guantanamo Bay prison. Thank you, President Obama!

As some of you are aware, I have returned to school and am studying for a graduate degree in international relations. An interesting course I took last year was entitled "A History of World Genocide." One of the texts for this course was *Ordinary Men*, by Christopher Browning. It tells the story of a German reserve police battalion, mostly comprised of rather ordinary working- and middle-class German citizens, that was mobilized to active duty during World War II. These reservists were neither Nazis nor SS troopers. Yet most of the reservists in this police battalion participated in some of the worst atrocities afflicted against the Jewish people living in Poland. The author tries to tell the story of this reserve police battalion from an unbiased perspective. In Browning's book, we follow the lives of several of the individuals assigned to this battalion, and we find that many of the police reservists were otherwise rather decent and caring individuals. Yet when ordered to participate in the torture and mass killing of innocent men, women, and children, the vast majority of the mobilized police reservists followed their orders. There were a few reservists who found ways to avoid participating in many of the atrocities, but they were the exceptions. The book is a frightening study in how ordinary people, under certain circumstances, can succumb to very evil behavior.

Included in my world genocide studies were tales of torture that included the Armenians by the Ottoman Turks; the Chechens-Ingush and the Crimean Tatars by the Soviet Union; Native Americans by the United

States Army and the Texas Rangers; the Rwandan Tutsis by the Rwandan Hutu; and the Serb Orthodox, Croatian Catholics, and Bosnian Muslims by one another following the break-up of Yugoslavia.

Had I visited Dachau at a younger age when I was much more naive about United States and world history, perhaps I would have had a different emotional reaction. Perhaps I would have seen Dachau as an anomaly in the history of human behavior. Perhaps I would have left Dachau with the question of *How?* How could human beings inflict such pain and suffering on other human beings? However, as I made my walk over the Dachau prison yard to board the bus for my return trip to Darmstadt, my question was *Why?* Why are humans capable of inflicting such pain and suffering on others?

January 2009.

29

Everyday Fear Factors of a Meat-Based Diet

I ONLY WATCHED ONE episode of NBC's *Fear Factor*. Once was enough! I found the show disgusting. Especially repulsive was a stunt requiring contestants to eat pastry filled with various live insects. Ugh!!

More grotesque than this stunt are the everyday fear factors associated with the meat-based diet of many humans. Consider the very real fear factors of those who choose to consume animal flesh:

FEAR FACTOR #1: GO TORTURE AND KILL A SENTIENT BEING!

Eight billion animals are killed for food every year in the United States alone. These are creatures with many of the same emotions and feelings as humans. Many of these farm animals would be loyal and loving pets if raised as such. Under the conditions of factory farming, animals suffer in crowded and filthy conditions until the terrifying day of their slaughter. By purchasing and consuming factory farm animal products, you are supporting this cruel, evil, and inhumane system.

FEAR FACTOR #2: HAVE SOME ANTIBIOTICS, HORMONE DRUGS, AND PESTICIDES WITH YOUR PASTRY!

Animals are pumped full of powerful antibiotics and hormone drugs to kill diseases resulting from filthy living conditions and to make them grow and produce faster. Most factory-farmed animals could not survive their concentrated living quarters were it not for heavy doses of antibiotics. These same drugs can be found in the meat you eat. Since pesticides become concentrated as they move up through the food chain, meat contains fourteen times the amount of pesticides as plant food. The full health impact upon humans of eating meat products laden with antibiotics and hormone drugs is unknown, but few doubt that these drugs have some serious negative consequences upon human health. It is known that the consumption of animal flesh with high levels of antibiotics results in the human body becoming increasingly resistant to antibiotic drugs used to treat various harmful bacteria.

FEAR FACTOR #3: INCREASE YOUR ODDS FOR DEVELOPING A CHRONIC OR LIFE-THREATENING DISEASE!

Overall, meat eaters have substantially increased risks for obesity, heart disease, high blood pressure, diabetes mellitus, osteoporosis, and some forms of cancer, particularly lung and colon cancer.

FEAR FACTOR #4: HELP STARVE A HUMAN CHILD!

Every two seconds a child dies somewhere in the world from starvation. Raising animals for food is an extremely inefficient way to feed a growing human population. The livestock population of the United States consumes enough grain and soybeans to feed over five times the entire human population of the country.

We feed farm animals eighty percent of the corn we grow and over ninety-five percent of the oats. It requires three-and-a-half acres to supply one person a meat-based diet for a year, whereas it only requires one-sixth of an acre to feed a human a vegetarian diet. If Americans reduced their meat consumption by only ten percent, it would free twelve million tons of grain annually for human consumption. This alone would be sufficient to feed each of the sixty million people who starve to death each year.

FEAR FACTOR #5: HELP DESTROY OUR PLANET!

You can't be an environmentalist and eat a meat-based diet. Over half of the water used in the United States is for growing livestock feed. It takes over one hundred times as much water to produce meat than to produce the nutritionally equivalent amount of wheat.

United States livestock produces 250,000 pounds of waste per second. This is twenty times more than humans produce. However, there are no sewage treatment facilities for this waste. Animal waste washed into our rivers and lakes causes increased nitrates, phosphates, ammonia, and bacteria. Oxygen content in water is decreased. Aquatic life is killed. The meat industry creates three times as much organic waste as all other U.S. industries combined.

The average animal-based diet in the United States generates the equivalent of about one and a half metric tons of carbon dioxide more per person per year than a plant-based diet yielding the same amount of calories. Livestock production alone contributes to eighteen percent of the global warming effect, which is more than every single car, train, and plane on Earth. Eating little or no meat is one of the easiest ways for individuals to reduce their environmental footprint and reduce greenhouse gases.

Who needs a reality-based television show to bring fear factors into our homes? Eating a meat-based diet is a very real and an everyday source of sufficient fear for those who choose such a diet. It has been eleven years since I made the conscious decision to follow a vegetarian diet. Going vegetarian has not only improved my health, but I now feel it was the best ethical and spiritual decision of my life. I encourage Unitarian Universalists (and those of other denominations and religious faiths) to consider the benefits of following a vegetarian diet. Can we really respect the interdependent web of existence of which we are all a part and not be vegetarian?

*Written in 2007 for the Unitarian Universalists
for the Ethical Treatment of Animals website.*

30

On the Eve of a Father's Birthday

IT WAS A BEAUTIFUL April morning. The preceding Sunday had been Easter. Trees and other plants were showing signs of new life following the dormancy of winter. Yet the fresh blades of grass emerging from the gravesite felt intrusive and disrespectful. It seemed as though the burial was only a week or so ago. Scanning the surrounding cemetery, I saw other graves more recent than his. As I read the name inscribed upon the neatly placed marker, tears flowed freely down my face. It was my first visit to my father's grave since his burial five months earlier. I thought, so this is what it's like to visit your father's grave. Scenes flashed through my mind of the many times I had been with parishioners as they returned to visit gravesites of loved ones. Momentarily, I wondered if what I was feeling was similar to what others felt when standing by the grave of a parent.

It was the evening of November 8, 1993, that I learned of my father's death. I had just sat down in the parsonage office of the Outlaw's Bridge Universalist Church, a rural parish located in the farmland of eastern North Carolina. I was in the final week of my ministry to this congregation. Cardboard boxes were scattered throughout the parsonage in preparation for the upcoming move to Clio, South Carolina, where I was to begin employment as a correctional chaplain at nearby Evans Correctional Institution. As I sorted through the day's mail, I flipped on my telephone answering machine to retrieve any messages. It was the same machine that often broadcasted my father's voice to me. The words that came over the speaker that evening tore at my gut. A tide of sadness and grief engulfed me. My legs went limp. My father was dead.

It was two days earlier that we had talked over that same phone. It had been one of our best telephone visits. My father had just returned to Waterloo, South Carolina, after a week of vacation at Myrtle Beach. We talked about his health. My father's health had deteriorated over the past two years due to heart and kidney disease. We talked about family, fishing at Myrtle Beach, issues in the ministry, and my upcoming employment as a correctional chaplain. With much excitement, I told him about the Victorian house I was in the process of purchasing in Clio, South Carolina. I jokingly told him that the living room in the old house was large enough for him to park his RV. He laughed and shared my enthusiasm. He was looking forward to making a trip to visit me after the move. My father was happy to know that I would be two hours nearer to him. We were both looking forward to being able to visit one another on a more frequent basis.

Words can't convey the sense of loss I felt at the time of my father's death. The events surrounding the funeral plans, family visitation, the funeral, and his burial seem like a blur to me. Although I've officiated at over a hundred funerals, it is all so different when you are the family member who is grieving. It is so different when you are the one sitting in one of the pews on the other side of the coffin. It is so different when you are among the family members sitting in the reserved seats placed under the funeral home canopy adjacent to the gravesite. These are memories you never forget.

My dad served for over thirty years as a United Methodist minister. Prior to his entering the ministry, he had worked at several occupations to include electrician, owner-operator of a country store, and salesman with Sears and Roebuck. He was in his midthirties when he answered what he felt was his "call to the ministry." It was not easy for him to return to college and seminary with a family that included three sons. But he did it! He was thirty-nine years old when he received his first parish appointment.

Dad and I had our differences, as I suppose all sons and fathers have at times. During my late adolescence and early adulthood, we often argued over religion. I don't know if my father ever fully understood my reasons for leaving the United Methodist Church and joining the Unitarian Universalist Association. I always had concern that my father felt some personal rejection with my decision. However, I think my father would have agreed that in the past several years we had come to share much in common concerning our views about God and religion.

I was proud that my father had once delivered the children's sermon at my Universalist church during one of his rare Sunday visits to see me. It was one of the few times that he ever heard me preach. Usually he was in his pulpit on Sundays and I was in mine. I don't recall the topic or theme of my sermon that Sunday, but I do remember my father telling me after the service how much he enjoyed my message. His compliment meant a lot to me!

The night following my father's funeral I was up late into the morning as I rummaged through my file cabinets searching for old photos and letters from my father. I came across a two-page handwritten letter that he wrote to me on September 29, 1991. The following lines are taken from that letter:

> I have a "gut" feeling that I should write you a letter. Many times a day I think of you and the good times I enjoyed with you. We had good times together and experiences no one can take from me. So much for the past. We can't relive the past, but we are still alive and the present and future are before us . . . now. I love you so very much!

I am writing this reflection the evening of May 28, 1994. Tomorrow would have been my father's seventieth birthday. I still have difficulty accepting his death. I often think of telephoning him but immediately realize I can't. I miss him very much.

We can never say "I love you" too many times to those whom we love. The present is all that we have. On the eve of his birthday, I am reminded once again of the brevity of life, the preciousness of time, and the priceless value of our relationships with one another.

31

Visit to a Kosovo Monastery

PATCHES OF SNOW REMAINED among the shadows of the monastery walls. Outside the monastery gate, the sound of rushing water was clearly audible from the nearby mountain stream as it made its way through Rugovo Gorge. I was standing in western Kosovo, only a few kilometers from the Montenegro border. The land in and around the stone structure has been considered holy ground since the thirteenth century. This had been the center for the Serbian Orthodox Church for centuries. The monastery is known as the Patriarchate of Pec. The chapel is actually a complex of four churches built between 1230 and 1330. It was my first visit to this religious site since my arrival in Kosovo on December 26, 2001.

Upon entering the stone structure, I was struck by the colorful religious icons adorning the chapel. Many of the icons were centuries old. There were hundreds of icons covering the stone walls. The smell of incense permeated the air. The sights and smell transposed me to a state of awe and reverence. I do love the feeling of being in a church of the Eastern Orthodox faith.

I purchased a votive candle from a nearby table and I carried the candle into one of the rooms within the chapel. I lit the candle for my deceased father and placed the candle in one of the votive stands. The flame from my candle joined the flames of several other candles. I wondered for whom the other candles burned.

As I walked across the monastery grounds, a small mongrel dog followed me. The dog had some resemblance to a beagle. The dog's tail was constantly wagging, and the dog seemed to smile at me. From the size of the dog's midsection, it was obvious that the dog was fed well. This was quite a contrast to some of the other dogs I had seen during my rides through rural Kosovo. Most of the dogs in Kosovo seemed to be skin and bone. A few days earlier I had witnessed several hungry dogs eating the carcass of a fellow canine that was lying on the roadside. What a blessing it must be to live the life of a monastery pet!

During my two-hour drive from Pristina to the Patriarchate of Pec, I passed through numerous war-torn villages. I noticed monuments to both Kosovo Serbs and Kosovo Albanians who had been killed in the recent fighting. I stopped at the site of a destroyed Serbian church. The church steeple was clearly visible in the rubble. According to Serbian Orthodox religious authorities, more than seventy Serb religious shrines, churches, and monasteries have been completed razed to the ground, damaged, or desecrated by Albanian extremists since the Kosovo Peacekeeping Force (KFOR) entered Kosovo in June of 1999. Many of the churches that remain are provided twenty-four-hour military security. Some of the churches are enclosed in razor wire fences complete with guard towers in which KFOR soldiers provide surveillance with fully loaded machine guns.

Upon arriving in Kosovo, I was surprised by the beauty of this land. Many of the mountain ranges are breathtaking to behold. The sunrises and sunsets are magnificent. The land is fertile. With the arrival of winter snow, much of Kosovo reminded me of western Colorado. Prior to the war, several ski slopes operated in the area. Kosovo is one of the more beautiful places I have ever visited.

The two primary religious faiths in Kosovo are Muslim and Serbian Orthodox Christian. Additionally, there are a small number of Catholic parishes. Approximately ninety percent of the population is Muslim. The Muslims are called the Kosovo Albanians. The Kosovo Albanians are quick to tell of the damage inflicted upon their people and their villages by the Serbs prior to the arrival of the KFOR peacekeepers. Each side has their stories of terror to tell. Fear and hate run deep. Hate continues to be a driving force in the lives of many of the people. Kosovo is a land of paradox: a land of despair and of hope; a land of scarcity and of rich resources; a land of hate and of love.

I am told that the Patriarchate of Pec Monastery was a sanctuary for both Muslims and Christians during some of the heaviest fighting in Kosovo. Standing within the monastery walls, I realized that unity can be found among those who choose peace despite the differences of religion; peace can be found despite a cultural history of discord; and an oasis of love can be found in a wilderness of hatred.

Spring 2002.

32

The Spirit of the First Christmas

IN MUCH OF EUROPE, the Christmas season is a time of festive lights, decorated trees, special holiday shopping markets, feasting, merriment, and parties. Downtown Heidelberg, Germany, is noted for their Christmas market, where vendors erect numerous decorative stalls to sell various Christmas gifts and other delicacies. Along the main walking street, colorful lights line the storefronts and most every store window has a beautifully decorated Christmas tree. The air is filled with the smells of cinnamon and mulled German wine. The sounds of recorded Christmas music gently flow from the various stalls and shops.

Much of the Christmas celebrations in Europe are not too unlike what can be found in cities and towns throughout the United States. The only major difference between Europeans and Americans at Christmas is that Europeans feel quite safe when walking their city streets after dark!

When we trace the origins of much of our modern-day Christmas culture, we find various sources. The ancient Romans held a festival called Saturnalia in December. Beginning on December 15, the Romans observed seven days of feasting, revelry, and merrymaking in honor of Saturn. Variations of the December Saturnalia festival eventually migrated throughout much of Western Europe and were always associated with indulgence of food and drink. From the ancient Persian religion of Zoroastrianism, we find the celebration of the god Mithra, god of light. This celebration of light was later associated with the winter solstice, which marked the beginning of lengthening daylight.

The origin of Santa Claus and gift giving can be traced to the altruistic bishop named Saint Nicholas who lived in Asia Minor, now known as Turkey, during the fourth century. Many years later much of Western Europe shared legends of a gift-bearing Saint Nicholas riding through the skies on a horse, often accompanied by an elf who whipped the children who misbehaved. The Dutch called Saint Nicholas *Sinterklaas*, and it is from the Dutch that we have Santa Claus in the United States. The Yule log came from Scandinavian mythology. In December a huge log was found and hauled into the house. The log was lit afire in honor of Thor, the Viking god of thunder and war. It was believed that Thor would bless the family with prosperity during the following year in reward for this ceremony.

The Christmas tree, mistletoe, and holly have German origins. These evergreens were brought into homes during the cold months of winter with the belief that they enhanced fertility. Thus, the American use of Christmas trees, mistletoe, and holly is from German traditions.

Probably the only aspect of modern Christmas culture that can be attributed to America is the increasingly materialistic aspect of this holiday time. Indeed, the Christmas shopping season, which now begins just after Halloween, is a "make or break" time for many American businesses. For most of Western civilization, the modern Christmas season is a joyous time of feasting, decorating, partying, and gift buying.

But what about those folks who can't participate in the festivities of our modern Christmas culture? It was a Saturday night in December 1994, and I was sitting in my study struggling to write a Christmas sermon for the inmates at the nearby state penitentiary where I was employed as chaplain.

I was feeling quite frustrated: How could I write and deliver a joyful Christmas message to a congregation of inmates, many of whom were serving long sentences and for whom family no longer existed?

There was no chapel at the prison. We used the visitation room for our chapel programs. Sunday worship services were scheduled to begin and end prior to the start of visitation at nine o'clock in the morning. As such, many inmates had to choose between having breakfast and going to chapel. There was a solitary artificial Christmas tree with a couple of branches missing, decorated with donated ornaments, in the visitation room. A few other festive Christmas decorations of snowmen, reindeer, and Santa Clauses adorned the walls of the room.

I often wondered if the tree and decorations did more emotional harm than good for the inmates. The decorations reminded each inmate of what he was missing "outside the wall."

I went back and reread the Christmas story from the Gospel of Luke. Joseph and the pregnant Mary were required to travel from Nazareth in

Galilee to Bethlehem to participate in a census. It was just Joseph and Mary. They left their families behind in Nazareth.

Once arriving in Bethlehem, they find that there is no lodging to be had or perhaps Joseph simply did not have funds for some of the more expensive rooms that might have been available. At this point, Mary begins to have labor pains. The only shelter they can find is in a stable. Among the sounds and smells of farm animals, they make their way along the stable pathway that is no doubt littered with animal manure. Mary's labor pains increase. Joseph desperately looks for some place for Mary to lie down other than the manure-covered ground, but he is not successful. From what we can discern from Luke's account, it appears that Mary gives birth while lying on the dirty ground. After the baby Jesus is born, Joseph locates a nearby feeding trough filled with fodder. It is in the manger that the newborn baby is laid to rest.

As my imagination pictured the actual scene of the first Christmas, it dawned on me that the inmates at the prison probably knew and understood the true "spirit" of that first Christmas much better than those of us who are caught up in the spirit of our modern Christmas culture.

The true spirit of that first Christmas was one of loneliness, despair, hopelessness, homesickness, degradation, and humiliation. There was the physical pain of childbirth for Mary and there was Joseph's emotional pain for not being able to do better for his wife and son. And there is no mention of a meal or food in Luke's account. Might we assume that both Mary and Joseph knew the pains of hunger during that night in the stable?

Once I made this connection, I felt a burst of energy and I rewrote my Christmas sermon. In my new sermon, I tried to help the inmates realize just how much they had in common with Joseph, Mary, and Jesus in the Bethlehem stable. There was nothing joyous and festive about that first Christmas.

The true spirit of the first Christmas was more akin to the spirit you find among inmates in prison, the homeless huddled under a bridge or waiting in a soup kitchen line at a homeless shelter, the unemployed family facing eviction from their home or apartment, the lonely man or woman in a nursing home for whom there are no family visits, the man or woman who can't afford needed medical care, the man or woman who is hungry and has no money for food, and the man or woman grieving the loss of a loved one.

If you wish to truly share in the spirit that was the first Christmas, stay away from the shopping malls, the festivities, and the partying. Go to where humans suffer. Go to where humans are marginalized from society. Go to those places where loneliness, despair, grief, hopelessness, homesickness, degradation, and humiliation are paramount.

Find those humans who suffer, and try and be with them in their suffering. Give of yourself to those who suffer. Here you will find the true spirit of the first Christmas. And if you can truly connect and help with the suffering of another, you will find an inner joy and meaning that far exceeds that which can be found in the festivities, partying, and materialism of our modern Christmas culture.

Written in November 2003 while on sixteen months of active duty as an army chaplain in Heidelberg, Germany.

33

Thanksgiving and Pilgrim Winters

FOR THOSE OF US living in the Northern Hemisphere of this planet, November is a harvest time. For those who live rural lifestyles, harvest time has always been a time of thanksgiving and celebration. In the United States, Thanksgiving Day is a time to remember our ancestors who came to this land on pilgrimages, endured severe difficulties, and gathered together after their first harvest to offer praise and thanksgiving for their survival in the wilderness.

One hundred and two persons set out on the Mayflower in September 1620, bound for the "Northern parts of Virginia" under the jurisdiction of the Virginia Company. On November 21 they cast anchor off Provincetown on the tip of Cape Cod. The gale winds of winter blew the Mayflower off course, driving the early Pilgrims toward the cold Massachusetts coast. Thus, it was necessary that they land at Plymouth and settle in this unknown territory.

It was a most difficult winter. The Pilgrims' greatest enemies were famine and sickness, causing the deaths of nearly half the entire company during that first winter. Parents lost children; children lost parents; husbands lost wives; wives lost husbands; brothers lost sisters; and sisters lost brothers. Records indicate that sometimes two or three persons died a day, and of the fifty survivors, in the time of most distress, there were but six or seven sound persons who fetched wood, made fires, dressed meat, made the beds, and washed the clothes of those others who were too sick to care for themselves.

After the horrors of the first winter, the spring and the local Native Americans were kind, and the Pilgrims were encouraged by the Indians to plant a variety of crops in considerable volume. It was after the fall harvest that the Pilgrims celebrated that first thanksgiving.

The essence of the first thanksgiving was the spirit of appreciation. It is appropriate that it is in nature's apparent November death that we acknowledge and affirm the spirit of appreciation. Late October and November is the time of the year when the green leaves of summer turn gold, scarlet, and orange. Autumn is a season of flaming colors. Botanists, however, tell us that the radiant color of autumn is that of a dying beauty. As the tree slowly diminishes the supply of water to its leaves, the green pigmentation resulting from chlorophyll is the first to break down, allowing the yellows and reds to become visible. These are yellow and red pigments that were as much a part of the leaves in April as in October, yet the colors are visible only in the process of dying. Are we not somewhat like a leaf? It often seems that the true colors of the human soul are most apparent as we face our deaths.

The Pilgrims of 1620 faced adversity, tragedy, loss, grief, hunger, sickness, and death before that first Thanksgiving. One could ask the question, would those early Pilgrims have experienced such a spirit of thankfulness for that first harvest had it not been for the previous winter? It seems to be human nature that we take so much for granted. Too often it is only after we have lost or almost lost someone or something in our life that we gain a true sense of appreciation.

It is in facing adversity, tragedy, loss, and even death that I call experiencing a "Pilgrim winter." And it is in surviving our "Pilgrim winter" that we gain a true sense of appreciation and thanksgiving. Must it take having a "Pilgrim winter" for us to experience a genuine sense of appreciation?

Many of you have known "Pilgrim winters," that is, the death of a loved one, disappointment in a relationship, serious illness or injury, and financial hardship, to name a few. Some of you are experiencing "Pilgrim winters" as you read this reflection.

Thanksgiving is not a November Mardi Gras. Although many Americans will feast on a delicious Thanksgiving Day meal, may we go beyond mere feasting. On this Thanksgiving Day may the spirit of appreciation be rekindled and manifested in our lives. Let us recall those lessons in appreciation that we learned following our previous "Pilgrim winters," and may we take a few moments to consider some of the many blessings that we have since taken for granted. May we reach out with love to those among us who may be experiencing their own "Pilgrim winters" this November. This is the true spirit of Thanksgiving.

*The above reflection was originally written as a homily for a 1987
Thanksgiving service at Anderson Street Chapel, Fort Jackson, South
Carolina. It was later revised as an article and appeared in several news-
papers and Universalist related publications.*

34

A Memorial Day Tribute

THERE ARE MANY STORIES as to the actual beginnings of Memorial Day. The first official observance was May 30, 1868, when flowers were placed on the graves of Union and Confederate soldiers at Arlington National Cemetery. Since World War I, Memorial Day has been commemorated as a day to honor all men and women who have died while serving in our nation's military.

War is a horror. May we never use Memorial Day as a time to glorify militarism or the killing and destructiveness of this human aberration we call war. We yearn for peace and we pray for the day when nations pursue understanding over violence in resolving disputes.

On this Memorial Day we remember our men and women in uniform whom we have loved and lost in service to our nation. We express gratitude for their lives and their sacrifices.

We also pause to express appreciation to those men and women who have served and who continue to serve in our nation's armed forces. May we give a special thanks to our Unitarian Universalist veterans on this Memorial Day. There are literally hundreds of Unitarian Universalists in our nation's armed forces today, and chances are, the individual sharing your Sunday pew was once in uniform. Please remember that many of our veterans continue to carry physical and emotional scars from their wartime service.

On this Memorial Day, I encourage Unitarian Universalists to pay tribute to those within our congregations who have died while in uniform, and may we honor our living veterans and military personnel. Regardless of your political views regarding war or a specific war, our members of the armed forces do not start wars nor do they dictate foreign policy.

This May, when you see Memorial Day flags flying in your towns, no matter what your feelings are about war, I hope you will remember the sacrifices made by our Unitarian Universalist veterans and military personnel. May we honor the lives of those who have died, and may we reach out in love to our living veterans and their families, extending the olive branch of acceptance and respect that our Unitarian Universalist faith calls us to embrace each and every day.

May 2007.

Bibliography

Ballou, Hosea. *A Treatise on Atonement*. Boston: Universalist Publishing House, 1882.

Bartlett, John. *Familiar Quotations*. Boston: Little, Brown & Company, 1980.

The Beacon Song and Service Book. Boston: Beacon Press, 1935.

Bellah, Robert N. et al. *Habits of the Heart*. New York: Harper & Row, 1985.

Booth, John Nicholls. *Introducing Unitarian Universalism*. Boston: UUA, 1981.

Borysenko, Joan. *Fire in the Soul*. New York: Warner Books, 1993.

———. *Guilt Is the Teacher, Love Is the Lesson*. New York: Warner Books, 1990.

Broecker, Wallace S., and Robert Kunzig. *Fixing Climate: What Past Climate Changes Reveal about the Current Threat—and How to Counter It*. New York: Hill and Wang, 2008.

Browning, Christopher R. *Ordinary Men*. New York: HarperCollins, 1992.

Buber, Martin. *I and Thou*. New York: Charles Scribner's Sons, 1970.

Buchholz, William M., MD. "The Medical Uses of Hope." *The Western Journal of Medicine* 148 (January 1988).

Butts, Thomas. *Tigers in the Dark*. Nashville: Abingdon, 1978.

Cassara, Ernest. *Universalism in America*. Boston: Beacon Press, 1971.

Ciardi John. "The Courage of his Confusion." *The Saturday Review*, June 2, 1962, 9.

Clark, Sergeant Major (Ret.) Shelby T. "Letters to the Editor" *Army Times*, June 17, 1991.

Cronin, A. J. *Adventures in Two Worlds*. Boston: Little, Brown & Company, 1952.

de Mello, Anthony, SJ. *Sadhana: A Way to God*. Garden City, NY: Doubleday Image Books, 1978.

———. *The Song of the Bird*. Anand, India: Gujarat Sahitya Prakash, 1982.

———. *Taking Flight*. New York: Doubleday, 1988.

Drummond, Henry. "Dealing with Doubt." In *Addresses*. Philadelphia: Henry Altemus Company, 1898.

Edwards, Tilden. *Spiritual Friend*. New York: Paulist Press, 1980.

Ehrenreich, Barbara. *Nickel and Dimed*. New York: Henry Holt & Co., 2001.

Eisnitz, Gail A. *Slaughterhouse*. Amherst, NJ: Prometheus Books, 1997.

Emerson on Man and God: Thoughts Collected from the Essays and Journals of Ralph Waldo Emerson. Mount Vernon, NY: Peter Pauper Press, 1961.

Foster, Richard J. *Celebration of Discipline*. San Francisco: Harper & Row, 1981.

Fox, Matthew. *Creation Spirituality*. San Francisco: Harper & Row, 1991.

———. *Original Blessing*. Santa Fe: Bear and Co., 1981.

Frankl, Viktor E. *Man's Search for Meaning*. Boston: Beacon Press, 1959.

Gellately, Robert, and Ben Kiernan, eds. *The Specter of Genocide*. New York: Cambridge University Press, 2003.

Gide, André. *If It Die*. New York: Vintage Books, 1935.

Hanna, Edward J. "Purgatory." *The Catholic Encyclopedia* [1914]. Reprinted: San Diego, Catholic Answers, 2007.

Harbury, Jennifer K. *Truth, Torture, and the American Way*. Boston: Beacon Press, 2005.

Harris, Glendon. *LectionAid*. Kamuela, HI: LectionAid, 1993, 1994 [quarterly publication].

———. *Pulpit Resource*. Honolulu, Hawaii: Pulpit Resource, Inc., 1991, 1992 [quarterly publication].

Heschel, Abraham Joshua. *Man's Quest for God*. New York: Charles Scribner's Sons, 1954.

Homes, Urban T. *Ministry and Imagination*. New York: Seabury, 1976.

———. *Spirituality for Ministry*. San Francisco: Harper & Row, 1982.

Howe, Charles A. *The Larger Faith: A Short History of American Universalism*. Boston: Skinner House, 1993.

Hymns for the Celebration of Life. Boston: The Unitarian Universalist Association, 1964.

IPCC, 2007: Summary for Policymakers. Climate Change 2007: The Physical Science Basis. Contribution of Working Group I to the Fourth Assessment Report of the Intergovernmental Panel on Climate Change. Cambridge University Press, Cambridge, United Kingdom and New York.

Kelly, Thomas. *A Testament of Devotion*. New York: HarperCollins, 1996.

Kempis, Thomas à. *The Imitation of Christ*. Brooklyn, NY: Confraternity of the Precious Blood, 1982.

Kennedy, Jay Richard. *Short Term*. Cleveland: World, 1959.

Kowalski, Gary. *The Souls of Animals*. Walpole, NH: Stillpoint Publishing, 1991.

Lao Tzu. *Tao Te Ching*. Translated by D. C. Lau. London: Penguin Group, 1963.

Lapoint, Justin. "Rekindling the Faith." *Universalist Herald* (Canon, GA), March 1992.

MacMillan, R. L., and K. W. Brown. "Cardiac Arrest Remembered." *Canadian Medical Association Journal* 104 (1971): 889–90.

Mattill, A. J. *A New Universalism for a New Century*. Gordo, AL: The Flatwoods Free Press, 1989.

McAleer, Neil. *The Cosmic Mind-Boggling Book*. New York: Warner Books, 1982.

Moltmann, Jürgen. *The Church in the Power of the Spirit*. New York: Harper & Row, 1977.

Moon, William Least Heat. *Blue Highways*. New York: Little, Brown & Company, 1982.

Moore, Thomas. *Care of the Soul*. New York: HarperCollins, 1992.

Morgan, John C. "Advice to Friends about Diversity." *Universalist Herald* (Canon, GA), August 1992.

Naimark, Norman M. *Fires of Hatred: Ethnic Cleansing in Twentieth Century Europe*. Cambridge: Harvard University Press, 2001.

Nierenberg, Danielle. "Eat Vegetables, Save Energy." *World Watch* 19, no. 4 (2006).

Nouwen, Henri J. M. *The Wounded Healer: Ministry in Contemporary Society*. New York: Image Books (Doubleday), 1979.

Parente, Alessio. *The Holy Souls*. Barto, PA: National Center for Padre Pio, Inc., 1990.

Peck, Scott. *A World Waiting to Be Born*. New York: Bantam Books, 1993.

Phelps, Norm. *The Longest Struggle: Animal Advocacy from Pythagoras to PETA*. New York: Lantern Books, 2007.

Potok, Chaim. *The Chosen*. New York: Simon & Schuster, 1967.

Relly, James. *Union*. London, 1782.

Robbins, John. *Diet for a New America*. Walpole, NH: Stillpoint Publishing, 1987.

Robinson, Elmo Arnold. *American Universalism*. New York: Exposition Press, 1970.

Robinson, Joe. *Work to Live*. New York: The Berkley Publishing Group, 2003.

Rosicrucian Manual. San Jose, CA: Supreme Grand Lodge of AMORC, 1978.

Savage, Charlie. *Takeover: The Return of the Imperial Presidency and the Subversion of American Democracy*. New York: Little, Brown & Company, 2007.

Seaburg, Carl, ed. *Great Occasions*. Boston: Beacon Press, 1968.

Sitler, Joseph. "When Death Serves Life." *Christian Century*, September 26, 1975.

Solzhenitsyn, Alexander. *The Gulag Archipelago*. New York: Harper & Row, 1973.

Southworth, Bruce. "What Does Spiritual Growth Mean, If Anything." In *1991 Selected Essays*. New York: UUMA, 1991.

Steere, Douglas V., ed. *Quaker Spirituality: Selected Writings*. Mahwah, NJ: Paulist Press, 1984.

Stone, Ronald H., ed. *Theology of Peace*. Louisville, KY: Westminster/John Knox, 1990.

Twain, Mark. *The Quotable Mark Twain: His Essential Aphorisms, Witticisms and Concise Opinions*. Edited by R. Kent Rasmussen. Chicago: Contemporary Books, 1997.

———. *The Unabridged Mark Twain*. Edited by Lawrence Teacher. 2 vols. Philadelphia: Running Press, 1976.

Tillich, Paul. *A History of Christian Thought*. New York: Simon & Schuster, 1968.

———. "The Right to Hope." In *Theology of Peace*, edited by Ronald Stone. Louisville, KY: Westminster/John Knox, 1990.

Tolstoy, Leo. *The Death of Ivan Ilyich*. New York: Random House (Bantam Classics), 2004.

Tsongas, Paul. *Heading Home*. New York: Alfred A. Knopf, 1984.

Tuttle, Will. *The World Peace Diet*. New York: Lantern Books, 2005.

Updegrave, Walter L. *We're Not in Kansas Anymore: Strategies for Retiring Rich in a Totally Changed World*. New York: Crown Business, 2004.

Vincent, Ken. "Dark Side STES." *Universalist Herald* (Dorchester, MA), May/June 2009, 14–17.

Vincent, Ken R., and John C. Morgan. "An 18th Century Near-Death Experience: The Case of George de Benneville." *Journal of Near-Death Studies* 25, no. 1 (2006): 35–48.

Walker-Riggs, Judith. Article in *First Days Record*, March 1992.

Weiss, Jess. *The Vestibule*. Port Washington, NY: Ashley Books, 1972.

Weitzner, Emil. "An Adaptation of Psalm 90." In *Great Occasions*, edited by Carl Seaburg, 259. Boston: Beacon Press, 1968.

Weston, Robert T. "Cherish Your Doubts." In *Hymns for the Celebration of Life*, compiled by the Unitarian Universalist Hymn Commission, 421. Boston: Unitarian Universalist Association, 1962.

———. "I Planted a Ripe Seed." In *Great Occasions*, edited by Carl Seaburg, 301. Boston: Beacon Press, 1968.

Wilbur, Earl Morse. *A History of Unitarianism in Transylvania, England, and America*. Boston: Beacon Press, 1969.

Williams, Redford. *Anger Kills: Seventeen Strategies for Controlling the Hostility That Can Harm Your Health*. New York: Random House, 1993.

About the Author

Floyd Vernon Chandler holds undergraduate degrees from Spartanburg Methodist College and Presbyterian College, graduate degrees from Emory University and Webster University, and a doctorate from Erskine Theological Seminary. He is currently pursuing graduate studies in international relations with the University of Oklahoma. He was ordained to the Unitarian Universalist ministry in 1976. Since his ordination, he has worked as a parish minister, an army chaplain, a college instructor, a correctional chaplain, a hospital chaplain, a community minister, and a mental health counselor. He was editor of the *Universalist Herald* from 1992 to 1998 and was chairperson of the Universalist Herald Publishing Company from 2004 to 2009. He is active with Unitarian Universalists for the Ethical Treatment of Animals (UFETA) and served on the UFETA board for over ten years. He is a Vanguard Member of People for the Ethical Treatment of Animals (PETA). He was one of the organizers of the first Universalist Convocation in 1990 and later served two terms as president of the Universalist Convocations. He was the recipient of the 2006 Heart of Universalism Award. He has served on the boards of the Mid-South and Thomas Jefferson districts of the Unitarian Universalist Association. He is retired from the U.S. Army Chaplain Corps with the rank of colonel, with over thirty-two years of combined active and reserve military duty. He currently is employed as a civilian with the U.S. Army's Family Advocacy Program, and his employment is recognized as a "community ministry" by the Unitarian Universalist Association's Department of Ministry.

Vernon, Nataliya, and Katerine Elizabeth reside in Trippstadt, Germany.